PUBLISHED

Shakespeare: *Henry IV Parts I and II* G.K. HUNTER
Shakespeare: *Henry V* MICHAEL QUINN
Shakespeare: *Julius Caesar* PETER URE
Shakespeare: *King Lear* FRANK KERMODE
Shakespeare: *Macbeth* JOHN WAIN
Shakespeare: *Measure for Measure* G.K. STEAD
Shakespeare: *The Merchant of Venice* JOHN WILDERS
Shakespeare: *A Midsummer Night's Dream* ANTONY W. PRICE
Shakespeare: *'Much Ado About Nothing' and 'As You Like It'* JOHN RUSSELL BROWN
Shakespeare: *Othello* JOHN WAIN
Shakespeare: *Richard II* NICHOLAS BROOKE
Shakespeare: *The Sonnets* PETER JONES
Shakespeare: *The Tempest* D.J. PALMER
Shakespeare: *Troilus and Cressida* PRISCILLA MARTIN
Shakespeare: *Twelfth Night* D.J. PALMER
Shakespeare: *The Winter's Tale* KENNETH MUIR
Shelly: *Shorter Poems and Lyrics* PATRICK SWINDEN
Spenser: *The Faerie Queene* PETER BAYLEY
Swift: *Gulliver's Travels* RICHARD GRAVIL
Tennyson: *In Memoriam* JOHN DIXON HUNT
Thackeray: *Vanity Fair* ARTHUR POLLARD
Trollope: *The Barsetshire Novels* T. BAREHAM
Webster: *'The White Devil' and 'The Duchess of Malfi'* R.V. HOLDSWORTH
Wilde: *Comedies* WILLIAM TYDEMAN
Virginia Woolf: *To the Lighthouse* MORRIS BEJA
Wordsworth: *Lyrical Ballads* ALUN R. JONES AND WILLIAM TYDEMAN
Wordsworth: *The Prelude* W.J. HARVEY AND RICHARD GRAVIL
Yeats: *Last Poems* JON STALLWORTHY

Drama Criticism: Developments since Ibsen ARNOLD P. HINCHLIFFE
Poetry of the First World War DOMINIC HIBBERD
Tragedy: Developments in Criticism R.P. DRAPER
The English Novel: Developments in Criticism since Henry James STEPHEN HAZELL
The Romantic Imagination JOHN SPENCER HILL
The Language of Literature NORMAN PAGE

TITLES IN PREPARATION INCLUDE

Defoe: *'Robinson Crusoe' and 'Moll Flanders'* PATRICK LYONS
T.S. Eliot: *Plays* ARNOLD P. HINCHLIFFE
Henry James: *'Washington Square' and 'Portrait of a Lady'* ALAN SHELSTON
O'Casey: *'Juno and the Paycock', 'The Plough and the Stars' & 'The Shadow of a Gunman'*
   RONALD AYLING
Yeats: *Poems, 1919–35* ELIZABETH CULLINGFORD
The 'Auden Group' Poets RONALD CARTER
Post-Fifties Poets: Gunn, Hughes, Larkin & R.S. Thomas A.E. DYSON

Poetry Criticism: Developments since the Symbolists A.E. DYSON
Comedy: Developments in Criticism DAVID PALMER
Medieval English Drama PETER HAPPÉ
Elizabethan Lyric and Narrative Poetry GERALD HAMMOND
The Pastoral Mode BRYAN LOUGHREY
The Gothick Novel VICTOR SAGE

The Language of Literature

A CASEBOOK

EDITED BY

NORMAN PAGE

MACMILLAN PRESS
LONDON

First published 1984 by
THE MACMILLAN PRESS LTD
London and Basingstoke
Companies and representatives throughout the world

Typeset by Wessex Typesetters Ltd
Frome, Somerset

Printed in Hong Kong

ISBN 0 333 34084 1 (hc)
ISBN 0 333 34086 8 (pbk)

CONTENTS

Part One: *Beginnings*

Part Two: *Language and Style: General Considerations*

Part Three: *Authors and Texts*

ACKNOWLEDGEMENTS

The editor and publishers wish to thank the following who have given permission for the use of copyright material: F. W. Bateson, extracts from *English Poetry and the English Language* (3rd edition 1973) by permission of Oxford University Press. Francis Berry, extract from *Poet's Grammar* (1958) by permission of Routledge & Kegan Paul Ltd. Cleanth Brooks, extract from *The Well-Wrought Urn* (1947) by permission of Dobson Books Ltd. John Russell Brown, extract from *Theatre Language* copyright © John Russell Brown (1972), reprinted by permission of Allen Lane/The Penguin Press Ltd. Anthony Burgess, extract from *Joystick* (1973) by permission of Andre Deutsch Ltd. Jonathan Culler, extracts from *Structuralist Poetics* (1975) by permission of Routledge & Kegan Paul Ltd. Donald Davie, extract from *Articulate Energy* (1955) by permission of Routledge & Kegan Paul Ltd. T. S. Eliot, extract from *On Poetry and Poets* (1957) reprinted by permission of Faber and Faber Ltd. William Empson, extract from *Seven Types of Ambiguity* (1930) by permission of Chatto & Windus Ltd. Bernard Groom, extracts from *The Diction of Poetry from Spenser to Bridges* (1955) by permission of the University of Toronto Press. A. E. Housman, extracts from *The Name and Nature of Poetry* (1933) by permission of Cambridge University Press. Randall Jarrell, extracts 'Texts from Housman' from *Kenyon Review*, 1, No. 3 (Summer, 1939) reprinted by permission of *Kenyon Review*. F. R. Leavis, extracts from *Revaluation* (1936) by permission of the Author's Literary Estate and Chatto & Windus Ltd. Vernon Lee, extract from *The Handling of Words* (1923) reprinted by permission of The Bodley Head. David Lodge, extract from *The Language of Fiction* (1966) by permission of Routledge & Kegan Paul Ltd. Professor Angus Mackintosh, for the article '*As You Like It*: A Grammatical Clue to Character' in *A Review of English Literature*, IV, 2 (1963) by permission of the author and the *Review of English Literature*. M. M. Mahood, extracts from *Shakespeare's Wordplay* (1957) by permission of Methuen & Co. Ltd. Sylvère Monod, extracts from *Dickens The Novelist* © (1968) University of Oklahoma Press, reprinted by permission of University of Oklahoma Press. Winifred Nowottny, extracts from *The Language Poets Use* (1962) by permission of Athlone Press Ltd. Norman Page, extract from *Speech in the English Novel* (1973) by permission of the Longman Group Ltd. and the author. Christopher Ricks, extracts from *Milton's Grand Style* (1963) by permission of Oxford University Press. George Rylands, extracts from *Words and Poetry* (1928) reprinted by permission of Chatto & Windus Ltd. John Spencer (editor), extracts from *Linguistics and Style* (1964) by permission of Oxford University Press. Caroline Spurgeon, extracts from *Shakespeare's Imagery and What it Tells Us* (1935) by permission of Cambridge University Press. Geoffrey Tillotson, extract from *Milton's Grand Style* Oxford University Press (1938) reprinted by permission of Mrs Kathleen Tillotson. George Watson, extracts from *The Study of Literature* (1969) reprinted by permission of A. D. Peters & Co. Ltd. Stanley Wells, extracts from 'Juliet's Nurse: The Uses of Inconsequentiality' in *Shakespeare's Styles*, P. Edwards, I. Ewbank and G. K. Hunter (editors), by permission of Cambridge University Press.

GENERAL EDITOR'S PREFACE

The Casebook series, launched in 1968, has become a well-regarded library of critical studies. The central concern of the series remains the 'single-author' volume, but suggestions from the academic community have led to an extension of the original plan, to include occasional volumes on such general themes as literary 'schools' and genres.

Each volume in the central category deals either with one well-known and influential work by an individual author, or with closely related works by one writer. The main section consists of critical readings, mostly modern, collected from books and journals. A selection of reviews and comments by the author's contemporaries is also included, and sometimes comment from the author himself. The Editor's introduction charts the reputation of the work or works from the first appearance to the present time.

Volumes in the 'general themes' category are variable in structure but follow the basic purpose of the series in presenting an integrated selection of readings, with an Introduction which explores the theme and discusses the literary and critical issues involved.

A single volume can represent no more than a small selection of critical opinions. Some critics are excluded for reasons of space, and it is hoped that readers will pursue the suggestions for further reading in the Select Bibliography. Other contributions are severed from their original context, to which some readers may wish to turn. Indeed, if they take a hint from the critics represented here, they certainly will.

A. E. DYSON

INTRODUCTION

That every work of literature, whatever else it may be, is a *verbal structure* is one of those truisms that has often been ignored and of which we need frequently to remind ourselves. As John Crowe Ransom wrote a generation ago: 'We should not discuss any art except in the presence of its shining reality, for fear that theory, which in this case is of spreading habit, will take us too far from our object and cause us to betray it.'[1]

Before we can interpret and evaluate any text, we have to understand it, in the fullest sense of that verb; and the process of understanding, often a complex business calling for flexibility, patience and tact, is likely to involve (among other things, and whether formally or informally) taking into account the way words are working. If description is not in itself criticism, it is at any rate part of the necessary activity that makes criticism possible. (Of course description can be an end in itself, as when a poem is dissected in order to demonstrate some aspect of linguistic behaviour: the poem in this instance is serving the same purpose as a non-literary text such as an advertisement or an insurance policy. This kind of activity, stopping short of interpretation and criticism, is not our concern in the present volume.)

Just as the serious study of how language works is a comparatively recent development, the notion that a legitimate way of approaching a text – whether it be *War and Peace* or an Edward Lear limerick – is to look closely at its language is a distinctively modern one, dating back (in the English tradition at least) no further than about 1920. This does not mean, of course, that before that date no-one looked closely at the language of literary works. Medieval scholars, for their own good reasons, scrutinised the language of Biblical and other texts, and a long tradition of classical scholarship and translation involved its practitioners in detailed attention to words. Literary criticism was not, however, usually part of their purpose. More relevant to our present concerns are the occasional asides of authors and critics mainly intent on other preoccupations – usually brief, throw-away observations that, however full of local insight, form part of no systematic attempt to engage in verbal description or analysis. Thus Samuel Johnson, in annotating passages from Shakespeare's plays, is sometimes impelled to comment in detail on points of language and style [*]; and Wordsworth, in attacking eighteenth-century poetic diction, quotes a sonnet by Gray in order to insist that only five of the fourteen lines are 'of any value', and that the reason for this is that 'the language of these lines does in no respect differ from that of prose'.[2]

In Part One of this selection, titled 'Beginnings', a few samples of this kind of early comment are assembled; the last, though dated 1933, is by a classical scholar representative of the older tradition. These are, after all, the exceptions that prove the rule: from Aristotle onwards, most literary critics until the present century concerned themselves with larger, more general and theoretical issues – such as the nature and function of literature, the definition of genres, and the morality of art.

In England the revolution in critical method came about in the years immediately following the First World War. Until that time the academic study of English had been largely dominated by philology and by literary history taught in very general terms. I. A. Richards (1893–1979), investigating the response of Cambridge students to texts from which evidence of authorship and date had been removed, found that many of them were incapable of independent critical reading and could only form a judgement about a particular text if they were informed in advance what was expected of them. In his *Practical Criticism* (1929) he documented this experiment, and 'practical criticism' – the detailed analysis of microtexts (short poems or extracts from longer works), paying attention to their internal features rather than to historical, biographical or other

* Here and elsewhere in the Introduction, an asterisk within square brackets indicates reference to material included in the relevant part of the Casebook. Numbered references to material or writers cited relate to the Notes at the end of this Introduction.

external considerations, and having as its objective evaluation as well as description – became a widely imitated pedagogical technique. In contrast to the amiable generalisations of traditional literary scholars, Richards's method was defiantly rigorous and scientific – or, as some would argue, pseudo-scientific, for its validity has since been called in question. As Ian Watt has said of practical criticism:

. . . both its pedagogical effects and its basic methodological assumptions seem to me to be open to serious question. For many reasons. Its air of objectivity confers a spurious authority on a process that is often only a rationalisation of an unexamined judgement, and that must always be to some extent subjective; its exclusion of historical factors seems to authorise a more general anti-historicism; and – though this objection is perhaps less generally accepted – it contains an inherent critical bias in the assumption that the part is a complete enough reflection of the literary whole to be profitably appreciated and discussed in isolation from its context.[3]

Watt goes on to argue that the techniques of practical criticism tend to favour certain kinds of writing, those that are 'richly concrete in themselves, stylistically brilliant, or composed in relatively small units', and that these techniques are better equipped to deal with verse than with prose, and notably ill-equipped to deal with extended forms such as the novel.

Be that as it may, as the influence of Richards spread from his pupils and imitators to *their* pupils and imitators, practical criticism had a profound effect on both the teaching of literature in universities and schools and the practice of literary criticism. It left its mark on a contemporary of Richards at Cambridge who was to become the most influential British critic of this century: F. R. Leavis (1895–1978), whose *New Bearings in English Poetry* (1932) and *Revaluation* (1936) apply its methods, with some modifications, to modern and traditional poetry, and who later turned his attention to the novel in *The Great Tradition* (1948), *D. H. Lawrence: Novelist* (1955), and (with Q. D. Leavis) *Dickens the Novelist* (1970). As a teacher and lecturer during a long career at Cambridge, and as a founder and editor of and leading contributor to the journal *Scrutiny* (1932–53), Leavis exerted a far-reaching influence. In *Revaluation* he restated the principle on which practical criticism rests:

In dealing with individual poets the rule of the critic is, or should (I think) be, to work as much as possible in terms of particular analysis – analysis of poems or passages – and to say nothing that cannot be related immediately to judgements about producible texts.   (pp. 2–3)

Both the strengths and weaknesses of the approach are to be detected in this sentence: the empirical method, properly intolerant of pretentious or banal generalisations that keep their distance from actual works of literature, can itself be exclusive or intolerant ('producible texts' amounting to texts the critic is prepared to produce), and the reference to 'poems or passages' hints at the limitations of the method when it comes to dealing with longer works.

Meanwhile, William Empson (born 1906), who had been a pupil of Richards at Cambridge, had published at a remarkably early age *Seven Types of Ambiguity* (1930), in which complexity and multiplicity of meaning were advocated as cardinal virtues of poetic language. Of Shakespeare's line (in Sonnet 73) 'Bare ruined choirs, where late the sweet birds sang', for instance, Empson writes:

. . . the comparison holds for many reasons; because ruined monastery choirs are places in which to sing, because they involve sitting in a row, because they are made of wood, are carved into knots and so forth, because they used to be surrounded by a sheltering building crystallised out of the likeness of a forest, and coloured with stained glass and painting like flowers and leaves, because they are now abandoned by all but the grey walls coloured like the skies of winter, because the cold and Narcissistic charm suggested by choir-boys suits well with Shakespeare's feeling for the object of the Sonnets, and for various sociological and historical reasons (the protestant destruction of monasteries; fear of puritanism), which it would be hard now to trace out in their proportions; these reasons, and many more relating the simile to its place in the Sonnet, must all combine to give the line its beauty, and there is a sort of ambiguity in not knowing which of them to hold most clearly in mind. Clearly this is involved in all such richness and heightening of effect, and the machinations of ambiguity are among the very roots of poetry.[4]

That last sentence could hardly have been written before about 1930: earlier generations, indeed, had been less ready to find 'richness and heightening of effect' in ambiguity than to follow Johnson in finding Shakespeare's wordplay 'poor and barren', a superficial and often tedious affair.

The emergence in America in the late 1930s of the so-called New Criticism was a development of the work of the British critics already referred to. John Crowe Ransom (1888–1974), Allen Tate (1899–1979) and Robert Penn Warren (born 1905) pioneered an anti-historical mode of criticism that stressed the self-sufficiency and autonomy of the text more than Leavis or Empson had ever done, and brushed aside the putative intentions of the author as irrelevant and indeed inaccessible. (This latter doctrine, the 'Intentional Fallacy', is propounded in W. K. Wimsatt and M. C. Beardsley's *The Verbal Icon* (1954); the essay in question had appeared somewhat earlier in the *Sewanee Review*.) In such widely influential works as Cleanth Brooks's *The Well Wrought Urn* (1947), irony, ambiguity and paradox were advocated as prime virtues of poetry – with, inevitably, the consequent tendency to undervalue those kinds of poetry whose strength lies in other directions.

This brief sketch of the development of Anglo-American criticism during the generation after about 1930 has offered no more than a bald indication of some of the most obvious landmarks. But it has perhaps sufficiently shown that, during the period in question, the language of literature became, almost for the first time, the object of close *critical* attention. It needs to be added that some permanently valuable work was done at the same time by scholars and critics who do not fit readily into the schools already described – for example, Caroline Spurgeon's remarkable investigations, published in the 1930s, into Shakespeare's imagery; and F. W. Bateson's account of poetic language (*English Poetry and the English Language*), which is rooted firmly in a literary-historical context and still makes illuminating reading after half a century.

On another scholarly front, the study of linguistics and stylistics was simultaneously developing apace. The founding father of modern linguistics is Ferdinand de Saussure (1857–1913), whose lectures at the University of Geneva in 1906–11 were published after his death from notes taken by his students as *Cours de linguistique générale* (1916; translated into English, 1959). Saussure's work represents a shift from the historical or *diachronic* approach to language to a sociological, structural, and *synchronic* approach; and, as George Watson has pointed out, 'it is clear that the extreme anti-historical bias of structural linguistics runs parallel to the mood called the New Criticism in English studies in the early twentieth century'.[5]

At one time it looked as though linguistics might provide valuable tools and a useful terminology for literary analysis; but with a few notable exceptions the marriage between these disciplines has been neither happy nor fruitful. To quote George Watson again:

If the cardinal question is posed: what literary work do we understand the better by reason of any discovery in the field of structural linguistics in the past half century? it is painfully clear that no highly convincing example can be presented. The revolution which has convulsed the study of language in the twentieth century has left the study of literary language almost untouched.[6]

More fruitful has been the tempering of New-Critical extremism with more traditional scholarly approaches; and some important work has been done that combines close attention to 'the words on the page' (that favourite Richards–Leavis war-cry) with the methods of historical criticism and structural analysis.

Most discussions of literary style, apart from the most general and theoretical, may be grouped under one or more of four main headings according to whether they emphasise or concentrate on (1) vocabulary and diction, (2) grammar and syntax, (3) imagery, (4) versification and such phonological elements as rhythm and onomatopoeia. (Often, of course, a single discussion may embrace more than one of these topics.) In all these areas major contributions have been made during the last half-century to our understanding of how language functions in a literary text.

1. *Vocabulary and diction.* One of the most obvious features of a writer's individual style – that quality which makes a passage by Milton or Hopkins, Jane Austen or D. H. Lawrence, immediately recognisable to those who have some acquaintance with their work – is his fondness for certain words or types of words. (A striking instance of this is the

correct identification by a Victorian reviewer, R. H. Hutton, of Trollope as the author of an anonymously-published novel [*] – all the more striking because Trollope has often been regarded as a writer whose style is not strongly idiosyncratic.) A moment's reflection reminds us that this is only an extension of the familiar phenomenon whereby we associate our friends and acquaintances, and perhaps especially our teachers, with certain characteristic locutions. We all have the same language at our disposal, but each of us makes his own unique selection from its resources. Linguists refer to this aspect of language – words considered separately as individual items – by the term *lexis*. *Diction* is sometimes used as a synonym for lexis or vocabulary (as in 'Milton's diction'), but perhaps would be more usefully confined to the more restricted sense of a stock language or idiom shared by many of the writers of a given period and involving a relatively narrow range of lexical resources (as in the phrase 'eighteenth-century poetic diction', used earlier in this Introduction). Samuel Johnson declared that 'Words too familiar, or too remote, defeat the purpose of a poet', and on these grounds objected to Shakespeare's use of *knife* ('an instrument used by butchers and cooks') in *Macbeth*. Wordsworth, rejecting the very notion of an exclusive diction, is prepared to call a spade a spade (and actually begins one poem 'Spade . . . !').

Donald Davie opens his *Purity of Diction in English Verse* (1952) by offering a serviceable piece of ground-clearing:

A friend asks me what I stand to gain from talking about 'the diction of verse', instead of 'the language of poetry'. For him, these are two ways of saying one thing, and my way is only the more pretentious. Now it seems to me that it would be pretentious to talk about the 'diction' of Gerard Manley Hopkins, and faintly precious, even, to talk of his 'verse'. If 'diction' is a selection from the language of men, then Hopkins may be said to use a poetic diction in the ridiculous sense that 'hogshead' or any other word one may call to mind was never used by him in any of his poems, and that he therefore used a selection of the language which excluded 'hogshead' or whatever word it is. But the point is that in reading the poems of Hopkins one has no sense of English words thrusting to be let into the poem and held out of it by the poet. One feels that Hopkins could have found a place for every word in the language if only he could have written enough poems. One feels the same about Shakespeare. But there are poets, I find, with whom I feel the other thing – that a selection has been made and is continually being made, that words are thrusting at the poem and being fended off from it, that however many poems these poets wrote certain words would never be allowed into the poems, except as a disastrous oversight. These different feelings we have, when we read English poetry, justify us in talking of the language of the one kind of poet, and the diction of the other kind, of the poetry of the one and the verse of the other.

We can, for example, properly speak of the diction of Gray, who strikes us as operating most of the time (like most of his contemporaries) within a restricted segment of the English vocabulary – so that the appearance of *stunk* in the last line of his fine poem 'On Lord Holland's Seat near Margate, Kent' administers a real shock.

The vocabulary of novelists has received a good deal of attention in recent years, especially since the publication of David Lodge's *Language of Fiction* (1966). W. T. Andrews has shown, for instance, that D. H. Lawrence is addicted to certain categories of words: among others, those suggesting 'nervous ill temper' (e.g., *irritably, fiercely, angrily, rage, resentment, exasperation*) and the habitual taunting of one character by another (*mocked, jeered, sneered, raillery, insisted, persisted*). Words of this kind are rare in Jane Austen, but she does make significant use (as Lawrence does not) of nouns and epithets designating moral qualities.[7] It goes without saying that such observations are not of much value in themselves but only in so far as they provide a solid basis for interpretation and criticism. Sylvère Monod's analysis of Dickens's vocabulary in *David Copperfield* [*] and Derek Bickerton's discussion of the language of Lawrence's *Women in Love* [*] show that particular works can be profitably examined in this way as well as by means of the familiar categories of structure, character, and so forth.

There are obvious dangers if description of vocabulary is allowed to become merely selective or impressionistic; and statistical methods have been widely used. Josephine Miles's very interesting work on the vocabulary of certain poets demonstrates that given words tend to recur in a way that seems to provide a clue to the predominant attitudes of the writer. (We may, for instance, ponder the fact that

Wordsworth is fond of the adjective *bright*, whereas Shelley uses *dark* with a higher than normal frequency.)[8] Recently there has been a considerable growth in the use of computerised methods for the investigation of literary style, and the availability of a concordance (either of a single work or of an author's entire corpus) is obviously a great boon to anyone engaging in the systematic study of vocabulary.[9]

In more specialised areas, there have been many studies of the use of regional dialects and other distinctive varieties of language – among others, of dialect in Shakespeare, Smollett, Dickens, Emily Brontë, George Eliot and Hardy.[10] This list reminds us again that, after a long period of neglect, the language of fiction has in the past generation become a popular and rewarding subject for study and analysis. As already indicated, the early advocates of 'practical criticism' and their American counterparts preferred to work with poetry rather than prose, and with short poems rather than long ones – partly because lyric poetry tends to exhibit the desiderated qualities (imagery, irony, ambiguity, paradox) in a more concentrated and convenient form, but also because no adequate methodology had been worked out for the close analysis of a long work such as a novel. Moreover, there still persisted a traditional assumption inherited from pre-twentieth-century critics that prose was inherently inferior to verse as a literary medium. The recognition of such novelists as Dickens and George Eliot as major writers by any standard has been accompanied by a vigorous interest in fictional style, and many of the major British and American novelists have been examined with special regard to their language.[11]

2. *Grammar and syntax.* An author's lexis – his individual choice from the stock of words available in his time, which may include archaisms, dialect, technical terms, slang, and even neologisms – is, of course, only one aspect of his language. Dictionaries, indispensable though they are, convey a false impression by treating words in isolation; for in practice words are used in conjunction with other words and acquire part of their meaning from the company they keep. With some authors, syntax may be at least as rewarding an object of study as vocabulary. The differences in the kinds of sentence-

patterns favoured by Samuel Johnson and Henry James, or Evelyn Waugh and Ernest Hemingway, reflect different attitudes to experience, for syntax is, as Tony Tanner has said, 'vision in action'. In this collection, the significance of poetic syntax in Milton and T. S. Eliot is suggested by, respectively, Christopher Ricks [*] and Donald Davie [*]. In a pioneering study of great interest, Francis Berry demonstrated that a specific grammatical feature may provide the substructure or groundplan for a poem such as Marvell's *To his Coy Mistress* [*]. Angus McIntosh's detailed analysis of pronouns in *As You Like it* [*] reminds us that such study needs to be based on an accurate knowledge of the grammatical and other conventions of the period in question. At their best, such approaches can be illuminating and can enable even the most familiar texts to be seen in a fresh way. (The reader who doubts this might try the experiment of reading Hardy's famous *Poems of 1912–13* with close attention to the tenses of the verbs.)

3. *Imagery* is a further element that has received close and sometimes systematic attention. The critics of the 1920s and 1930s who regarded compactness of expression and density of meaning as prime poetic virtues naturally held metaphor and other forms of imagery in high esteem, since they are devices for saying much in little. (William Empson's comment on a line from Shakespeare's Sonnet 73, already quoted, is a notable case in point.) Between the wars, Caroline Spurgeon and others exhaustively enumerated and classified the imagery of Shakespeare's plays. Though Professor Spurgeon's methods and conclusions can be criticised, her accounts of such patterns as the recurrent imagery of disease in *Hamlet* [*] and the 'cosmic' imagery of *Antony and Cleopatra* still make rewarding reading. Nor is imagery of importance only in poetry and poetic drama: in novels and short stories it can be used both for local effect and, more ambitiously, as a stucturing device. The importance of repetition in fiction, on the various levels of key-words, allusions, and images, has been stressed by David Lodge [*] and others.

4. *Versification, rhythm etc.* Literature – prose as well as verse – demands to be heard as well as seen, even if the 'hearing' takes place only within the reader's head. No discussion of the

resources of literary language is complete without some reference to the dimensions of word or sentence that relate to their auditory effect: the combination and repetition of the sounds of vowels and consonants; the tempo and inflection that the words impose upon the sensitive reader; the rhythm (whether highly-patterned, as in most verse, or more irregular, as in most prose). The analysis of poetry often requires that careful scrutiny be given to these elements. Consider, for example, in this volume, Geoffrey Tillotson's provocative comments on the differing use of onomatopoeia in Pope and Tennyson [*]; and Randall Jarrell's meticulous examination of the precise tone of the apparently unremarkable phrase 'Not me' in a poem by Housman [*]. As John Russell Brown's discussion of the language of Harold Pinter shows, however, prose may also repay similar attention [*]; and the language of, say, Dickens or Joyce or Beckett can hardly be adequately described without some analysis of its auditory qualities.

The first group of extracts in this selection, 'Beginnings', has been described above. The second deals with such general topics as the analysis of style, the differences between verse and prose, the importance of sound in poetry, the nature of dialogue in fiction, and the role of syntax and repetition in literary discourse.

The third and longest section consists of a series of more specific discussions of individual authors and texts from Shakespeare to the present day, representing the work of critics of the past fifty years as well as a variety of approaches (via diction, syntax, imagery, and so on). Some of the extracts form part of an argument developed at much greater length, and the interested reader may wish to look up the discussions in their original contexts.

The juxtaposition of extracts exemplifying different kinds of approach to similar material is intended to suggest that a variety of methods may all have their distinctive advantages and make their own contribution to the fuller understanding of a work of literature. Thus, contrasting approaches to Shakespeare and to the language of a novel are presented both for their intrinsic and for their contrastive interest. Many of these case-studies may not only be found of interest in their own right but serve as models for similar explorations of other texts.

NOTES

1. John Crowe Ransom, 'The Understanding of Fiction', *Kenyon Review*, XII (1950), p. 194.

2. William Wordsworth, Preface to the Second Edition of *Lyrical Ballads* (1800).

3. Ian Watt, 'The First Paragraph of *The Ambassadors*: An Explication', *Essays in Criticism*, X (1960), p. 251.

4. William Empson, *Seven Types of Ambiguity* (London, 1930; third edition, 1963), pp. 2–3.

5. George Watson, *The Study of Literature* (London, 1969), p. 143.

6. Ibid., p. 152.

7. W. T. Andrews, 'D. H. Lawrence's Favourite Jargon', *Notes and Queries*, n.s. XIII (1966), pp. 97–8; Norman Page, *The Language of Jane Austen* (Oxford, 1972).

8. See Josephine Miles, *Wordsworth and the Vocabulary of Emotion* (Berkeley, Cal., 1942); *Major Adjectives in English Poetry from Wyatt to Auden* (Berkeley, Cal., 1946); *The Primary Language of Poetry in the 1740s and 1840s* (Berkeley, Cal., 1950); *The Primary Language of Poetry in the 1940s* (Berkeley, Cal., 1951).

9. See Alan Jones and R. F. Churchhouse (eds.), *The Computer in Literary and Linguistic Studies* (Cardiff, 1976); D. E. Ager, F. E. Knowles, and Joan Smith (eds.), *Advances in Computer-Aided Literary and Linguistic Research* (London, 1979).

10. See, for example, H. Kökeritz, 'Shakespeare's Use of Dialect', *Transactions of the Yorkshire Dialect Society*, LI (1951), pp. 10–25; W. A. Boggs, 'Dialectal Ingenuity in *Humphry Clinker*', *Papers on English Language and Literature*, I (1965), pp. 327–37; Norman Page, 'Convention and Consistency in Dickens' Cockney Dialect', *English Studies*, LI (1970), pp. 339–44; C. Dean, 'Joseph's Speech in *Wuthering Heights*', *Notes and Queries*, n.s. VII (1960), pp. 73–6; P. Ingham, 'Dialect in the Novels of Hardy and George Eliot, in G. Watson (ed.), *Literary English Since Shakespeare* (London, 1970), pp. 347–63.

11. See, for example, K. C. Phillipps, *Jane Austen's English* (London, 1970); John W. Clark, *The Language and Style of Anthony Trollope* (London, 1975); G. L. Brook, *The Language of Dickens* (London, 1970); Seymour Chatman, *The Later Style of Henry James* (Oxford, 1972).

PART ONE
Beginnings

Sir Philip Sidney   (1595)

'English as a Medium for Poetry'

. . . Now, of versifying there are two sorts, the one ancient, the other modern; the ancient marked the quantity of each syllable, and according to that framed his verse; the modern, observing only number, with some regard of the accent, the chief life of it standeth in that like sounding of the words, which we call rhyme. Whether of these be the more excellent, would bear many speeches; the ancient, no doubt, more fit for music, both words and time observing quantity; and more fit lively to express divers passions, by the low or lofty sound of the well-weighed syllable. The latter, likewise, with his rhyme striketh a certain music to the ear; and, in fine, since it doth delight, though by another way, it obtaineth the same purpose; there being in either, sweetness, and wanting in neither, majesty. Truly the English, before any vulgar language I know, is fit for both sorts; for, for the ancient, the Italian is so full of vowels, that it must ever be cumbered with elisions. The Dutch[1] so, of the other side, with consonants, that they cannot yield the sweet sliding fit for a verse. The French, in his whole language, hath not one word that hath his accent in the last syllable, saving two, called antepenultima; and little more hath the Spanish; and therefore very gracelessly may they use dactiles. The English is subject to none of these defects.

Now for rhyme, though we do not observe quantity, we observe the accent very precisely, which other languages either cannot do, or will not do so absolutely. That 'caesura', or breathing-place, in the midst of the verse, neither Italian nor Spanish have, the French and we never almost fail of. Lastly, even the very rhyme itself the Italian cannot put in the last syllable, by the French named the masculine rhyme, but still in the next to the last, which the French call the female; or the next before that, which the Italian calls 'sdrucciola';[2] the example of the former is, 'buono', 'suono'; of the sdrucciola is, 'femina', 'semina'. The French, of the other side, hath both the male, as 'bon', 'son', and the female, as 'plaise', 'taise'; but the 'sdrucciola' he hath not; where the English hath all three, as 'due', 'true', 'father', and 'rather', 'motion',[3] 'potion'; with much more which might be said, but that already I find the trifling of this discourse is much too much enlarged. . . .

SOURCE: extract from *The Apologie for Poetrie* (entitled in some editions *The Defence of Poesy*), written about 1580, but published posthumously in 1595.

NOTES

1. [Ed.] 'Dutch': used generically by Sidney of all the varieties of German in his day (cf. 'Deutsch').
2. That is, the easy sliding of words of three or more syllables. [Note in an early edition.]
3. [Ed.] Sidney clearly here intends the Elizabethan pronunciation: 'mo–ti–on' etc.

Alexander Pope   (1711)

'The Externals of Verse'

. . .

But most by Numbers judge a Poet's Song,
And smooth or rough, with them, is right or wrong;
In the bright Muse tho' thousand Charms conspire,
Her Voice is all these tuneful Fools admire,
Who haunt Parnassus but to please their Ear,
Not mend their Minds; as some to Church repair,
Not for the Doctrine, but the Musick there.

These Equal Syllables alone require,
Tho' oft the Ear the open Vowels tire,
While Expletives their feeble Aid do join,
And ten low Words oft creep in one dull Line,
While they ring round the same unvary'd Chimes,
With sure Returns of still expected Rhymes.
Where'e'er you find the cooling Western Breeze,
In the next Line, it whispers thro' the Trees;
If Chrystal Streams with pleasing Murmurs creep,
The Reader's threatened (not in vain) with Sleep.
Then, at the last, and only Couplet fraught
With some unmeaning Thing they call a Thought,
A needless Alexandrine ends the Song,
That like a wounded Snake, drags it slow length along.
Leave such to tune their own dull Rhimes, and know
What's roundly smooth, or languishingly slow;
And praise the Easie Vigor of a Line,
Where Denham's Strength, and Waller's Sweetness join.
True Ease in Writing comes from Art, not Chance,
As those move easiest who have learn'd to dance.
'Tis not enough no Harshness gives Offence,
The Sound must seem an Eccho to the Sense.
Soft is the Strain when Zephyr gently blows,
And the smooth Stream in smoother Numbers flows;
But when loud Surges lash the sounding Shore,
The hoarse, rough Verse shou'd like the Torrent roar.
When Ajax strives, some Rock's vast Weight to throw,
The Line too labours, and the Words move slow;
Not so, when swift Camilla scours the Plain,
Flies o'er th'unbending Corn, and skims along the Main.
. . .

SOURCE: excerpt from *An Essay on Criticism* (1711), lines 337–73.

Joseph Addison   (1712)

'The Language of *Paradise Lost*'

. . .

Having already treated of the Fable, the Characters and
Sentiments in the *Paradise Lost*, we are in the last Place to
consider the *Language*; and as the learned World is very much
divided upon *Milton* as to this Point, I hope they will excuse me
if I appear particular in any of my Opinions, and encline to
those who judge the most advantagiously of the Author.

It is requisite that the Language of an Heroic Poem should
be both Perspicuous and Sublime. In Proportion as either of
these two Qualities are wanting, the Language is imperfect.
Perspicuity is the first and most necessary Qualification;
insomuch that a good-natur'd Reader sometimes overlooks a
little Slip even in the Grammar or Syntax, where it is
impossible for him to mistake the Poet's Sense. Of this kind is
that Passage in *Milton*, wherein he speaks of *Satan*.

> God and his Son except,
> Created thing nought valu'd he nor shunn'd.   [II 678–9]

And that in which he describes *Adam* and *Eve*.

> *Adam* the goodliest Man of Men since born
> His Sons, the fairest of her Daughters *Eve*.   [IV 323–4]

It is plain, that in the former of these Passages, according to
the natural Syntax, the Divine Persons mentioned in the first
Line are represented as created Beings; and that in the other,
Adam and *Eve* are confounded with their Sons and Daughters.
Such little Blemishes as these, when the Thought is great and
natural, we should, with *Horace*, impute to a pardonable
Inadvertency, or to the Weakness of Human Nature, which
cannot attend to each minute Particular, and give the last
finish to every Circumstance in so long a Work. The Ancient

Criticks therefore, who were acted by a Spirit of Candour, rather than that of Cavilling, invented certain Figures of Speech, on purpose to palliate little Errors of this Nature in the Writings of those Authors who had so many greater Beauties to attone for them.

If Clearness and Perspicuity were only to be consulted, the Poet would have nothing else to do but to cloath his Thoughts in the most plain and natural Expressions. But since it often happens that the most obvious Phrases, and those which are used in ordinary Conversation, become too familiar to the Ear, and contract a kind of Meanness by passing through the Mouths of the Vulgar, a Poet should take particular Care to guard himself against Idiomatick Ways of speaking. *Ovid* and *Lucan* have many Poornesses of Expression upon this account, as taking up with the first Phrases that offered, without putting themselves to the Trouble of looking after such as would not only be natural, but also elevated and sublime. *Milton* has but a few Failings in this kind, of which, however, you may meet with some Instances, as in the following Passages [Addison quotes III 474–6; V 395–7; X 733–6]. The great Masters in Composition know very well that many an elegant Phrase becomes improper for a Poet or an Orator, when it has been debased by common Use. For this Reason the Works of Antient Authors, which are written in dead Languages, have a great Advantage over those which are written in Languages that are now spoken. Were there any Mean Phrases or Idioms in *Virgil* and *Homer*, they would not shock the Ear of the most delicate Modern Reader, so much as they would have done that of an old *Greek* or *Roman*, because we never hear them pronounced in our Streets, or in ordinary Conversation.

It is not therefore sufficient, that the Language of an Epic Poem be Perspicuous, unless it be also Sublime. To this End it ought to deviate from the common Forms and ordinary Phrases of Speech. The Judgment of a Poet very much discovers it self in shunning the common Roads of Expression, without falling into such ways of Speech as may seem stiff and unnatural; he must not swell into a false Sublime, by endeavouring to avoid the other Extream. Among the *Greeks,* *Aeschylus*, and some times *Sophocles* were guilty of this

Fault; among the *Latins*, *Claudian* and *Statius*; and among our own Countrymen, *Shakespear* and *Lee*. In these Authors the Affectation of Greatness often hurts the Perspicuity of the Stile, as in many others the Endeavour after Perspicuity prejudices its Greatness.

Aristotle has observed, that the Idiomatick Stile may be avoided, and the Sublime formed, by the following Methods. First, by the Use of Metaphors: such are those in *Milton*,

Imparadised in anothers Arms,   [IV 506]

        And in his Hand a Reed
Stood waving *tipt* with Fire;   [VI 579–80]

The grassie Clods now *calv'd*.   [VII 463]

Spangled with eyes . . .   [IX 130]

In these and innumerable other Instances, the Metaphors are very bold but just; I must however observe, that the Metaphors are not thick sown in *Milton*, which always savours too much of Wit; that they never clash with one another, which as Aristotle observes, turns a Sentence into a Kind of an Enigma or Riddle; and that he seldom has Recourse to them where the proper and natural Words will do as well.

Another way of raising the Language, and giving it a Poetical Turn, is to make Use of the Idioms of other Tongues. *Virgil* is full of the *Greek* Forms of Speech, which the Criticks call *Hellenisms*, as *Horace* in his Odes abounds with them much more than *Virgil*. I need not mention the several Dialects which *Homer* has made use of for this End. *Milton* in Conformity with the Practice of the Ancient Poets, and with *Aristotle*'s Rule, has infused a great many *Latinisms* as well as *Graecisms*, and sometimes *Hebraisms*, into the Language of his Poem; . . .

Under this Head may be reckoned the placing the Adjective after the Substantive, the Transposition of Words, the turning the Adjective into a Substantive, with several other Foreign Modes of Speech, which this Poet has naturalized to give his Verse the greater Sound, and throw it out of Prose.

The third Method mentioned by *Aristotle*, is what agrees with the Genius of the *Greek* Language more than with that of any other Tongue, and is therefore more used by *Homer* than by any other Poet. I mean the lengthening of a Phrase by the Addition of Words, which may either be inserted or omitted, as also by the extending or contracting of particular Words by the Insertion or Omission of certain Syllables. *Milton* has put in practice this Method of raising his Language, as far as the Nature of our Tongue will permit, as in the Passage above-mentioned, *Eremite*, for what is Hermite, in common Discourse. If you observe the Measure of his Verse, he has with great Judgment suppressed a Syllable in several Words, and shortened those of two Syllables into one, by which Method, besides the above-mentioned Advantage, he has given a greater Variety to his Numbers. But this Practice is more particularly remarkable in the Names of Persons and of Countries, as *Beëlzebub*, *Hessebon*, and in many other Particulars, wherein he has either changed the Name, or made use of that which is not the most commonly known, that he might the better depart from the Language of the Vulgar.

The same Reason recommended to him several old Words, which also makes his Poem appear the more venerable, and gives it a greater Air of Antiquity.

I must likewise take notice, that there are in *Milton* several Words of his own Coining, as *Cerberean, miscreated, hell-doom'd, Embryon* Atoms, and many others. If the Reader is offended at this Liberty in our *English* Poet, I would recommend him to a Discourse in *Plutarch*, which shews us how frequently *Homer* has made use of the same Liberty.

Milton by the above-mentioned Helps, and by the Choice of the noblest Words and Phrases which our Tongue would afford him, has carried our Language to a greater height than any of the *English* Poets have ever done before or after him, and made the Sublimity of his Stile equal to that of his Sentiments,

I have been the more particular in these Observations on *Milton*'s *Stile*, because it is that part of him in which he appears the most singular. The Remarks I have here made upon the Practice of other Poets, with my Observations out of *Aristotle*, will perhaps alleviate the Prejudice which some have taken to his Poem upon this Account; tho' after all, I must confess, that I think his Stile, tho' admirable in general, is in some places too much stiffened and obscured by the frequent Use of those Methods, which *Aristotle* has prescribed for the raising of it.

This Redundancy of those several Ways of Speech which *Aristotle* calls *foreign Language*, and with which *Milton* has so very much enriched, and in some places darkened the Language of his Poem, was the more proper for his use, because his Poem is written in Blank Verse. Rhyme, without any other Assistance, throws the Language off from Prose, and very often makes an indifferent Phrase pass unregarded; but where the Verse is not built upon Rhymes, there Pomp of Sound, and Energy of Expression, are indispensably necessary to support the Stile, and keep it from falling into the Flatness of Prose.

Those who have not a Taste for this Elevation of Stile, and are apt to ridicule a Poet when he goes out of the common Forms of Expression, would do well to see how *Aristotle* has treated an Ancient Author, called *Euclid*, for his insipid Mirth upon this Occasion. Mr. *Dryden* used to call this sort of Men his Prose-Criticks.

I should, under this Head of the Language, consider *Milton*'s Numbers, in which he has made use of several Elisions, that are not customary among other *English* Poets, as may be particularly observed in his cutting off the Letter *Y*, when it precedes a Vowel. This, and some other Innovations in the Measure of his Verse, has varied his Numbers, in such a manner as makes them incapable of satiating the Ear and cloying the Reader, which the same uniform Measure would certainly have done, and which the perpetual Returns of Rhyme never fail to do in long Narrative Poems. I shall close these Reflections upon the Language of *Paradise Lost*, with observing that *Milton* has copied after *Homer*, rather than *Virgil*, in the length of his Periods, the Copiousness of his Phrases, and the running of his Verses into one another.

SOURCE: from *The Spectator*, No. 285 (26 January 1712). This is the third of eighteen essays by Addison on *Paradise Lost*.

Thomas Gray   (1742)

'The Language of Poetry'

. . . As to matter of stile, I have this to say: The language of
the age is never the language of poetry; except among the
French, whose verse, where the thought or image does not
support it, differs in nothing from prose. Our poetry, on the
contrary, has a language peculiar to itself; to which almost
every one, that has written, has added something by enriching
it with foreign idioms and derivatives: Nay sometimes words
of their own composition or invention. Shakespear* and
Milton have been great creators this way; and no one more
licentious than Pope or Dryden, who perpetually borrow
expressions from the former. Let me give you some instances
from Dryden, whom every body reckons a great master of our
poetical tongue, – Full of *museful mopeings* – unlike the *trim* of
love – a pleasant *beverage* – a *roundelay* of love – stood silent in
his *mood* – with knots and *knares* deformed – his *ireful mood* – in
proud *array* – his *boon* was granted – and *disarray* and shameful
rout – *wayward* but wise – *furbished* for the field – the *foiled
dodderd* oaks – *disherited* – *smouldring* flames – *retchless* of laws –
crones old and ugly – the *beldam* at his side – the *grandam-
hag* – *villanize* his Father's fame. – But they are infinite: and
our language not being a settled thing (like the French) has an
undoubted right to words of an hundred years old, provided
antiquity have not rendered them unintelligible. In truth,
Shakespeare's language is one of his principal beauties; and he
has no less advantage over your Addisons and Rowes in this,
than in those other great excellencies you mention. Every word
in him is a picture. Pray put me the following lines into the
tongue of our modern Dramatics:

---

* [Ed.] Gray's original spelling is here retained.

> But I, that am not shaped for sportive tricks,
> Nor made to court an amorous looking-glass:
> I, that am rudely stampt, and want love's majesty
> To strut before a wanton ambling nymph;
> I, that am curtail'd of this fair proportion,
> Cheated of feature by dissembling nature,
> Deform'd, unfinish'd, sent before my time
> Into this breathing world, scarce half made up,
>
> [*Richard III*, I i 14–21]

And what follows. To me they appear untranslatable; and if this be the case, our language is greatly degenerated. . . .

SOURCE: extract from a letter to Richard West (8 April 1742);reproduced in Paget Toynbee and L. Whibley (eds), *Correspondence of Thomas Gray*, 3 vols; revised H. W. Starr (Oxford, 1971).

Samuel Johnson (1765)

'Three Notes on Shakespeare'

[*King Lear*, IV i 68–9]

> Let the superfluous and lust-dieted man,
> That slaves your ordinance,

The language of Shakespeare is very licentious, and his words have often meanings remote from the proper and original use. To *slave* or *beslave* another is to *treat* him *with terms of indignity*; in a kindred sense, to *slave the ordinance*, may be, *to* slight *or* ridicule *it*.

[*Macbeth*, II iii 118–21]

> Here, lay Duncan;
> His silver skin laced with his golden blood,
> And his gash'd stabs look'd like a breach in nature
> For Ruin's wasteful entrance.

Mr Pope has endeavoured to improve one of these lines by substituting *goary blood* for *golden blood*; but it may easily be admitted that he who could on such an occasion talk of *lacing the silver skin*, would *lace it* with *golden blood*. No amendment can be made to this line, of which every word is equally faulty, but by a general blot.

It is not improbable, that Shakespeare put these forced and unnatural metaphors into the mouth of Macbeth as a mask of artifice and dissimulation, to show the difference between the studied language of hypocrisy, and the natural outcries of sudden passion. This whole speech so considered, is a remarkable instance of judgment, as it consists entirely of antithesis and metaphor.

[*Hamlet*, V ii 41–2]

> As Peace should still her wheaten garland wear,
> And stand a comma 'tween their amities;

The expression of our authour is, like many of his phrases, sufficiently constrained and affected, but it is not incapable of explanation. The *Comma* is the note of *connection* and continuity of sentences; the *Period* is the note of *abruption* and disjunction. Shakespeare had it perhaps in his mind to write, That unless England complied with the mandate, *war should put a* period *to their amity*; he altered his mode of diction, and thought that, in an opposite sense, he might put, That *Peace should stand a* Comma *between their amities*. This is not an easy style; but is it not the style of Shakespeare?

SOURCE: extracts from *The Plays of William Shakespeare, in Eight Volumes, with the Corrections and Illustrations of Various Commentators; To which are added Notes by Sam. Johnson* (1765). Walter Raleigh's *Johnson on Shakespeare* (1908) contains a useful selection from the notes.

William Wordsworth   (1800)

'Poetic Diction'

. . . Perhaps in no way, by positive example, could more easily be given a notion of what I mean by the phrase *poetic diction* than by referring to a comparison between the metrical paraphrases which we have of passages in the Old and New Testament, and those passages as they exist in our common Translation. . . . By way of immediate example, take the following of Dr Johnson:

> Turn on the prudent Ant thy heedless eyes,
> Observe her labours, Sluggard, and be wise;
> No stern command, no monitory voice,
> Prescribes her duties, or directs her choice;
> Yet, timely provident, she hastes away
> To snatch the blessings of a plenteous day;
> When fruitful Summer loads the teeming plain,
> She crops the harvest, and she stores the grain.
> How long shall sloth usurp thy useless hours,
> Unnerve thy vigour, and enchain thy powers?
> While artful shades thy downy couch enclose,
> And soft solicitation courts repose,
> Amidst the drowsy charms of dull delight,
> Year chases year with unremitted flight,
> Till Want now following, fraudulent and slow,
> Shall spring to seize thee, like an ambush'd foe.

From this hubbub of words pass to the original. 'Go to the Ant, thou Sluggard, consider her ways, and be wise: which having no guide, overseer, or ruler, provideth her meat in the summer, and gathereth her food in the harvest. How long wilt thou sleep, O Sluggard? when wilt thou arise out of thy sleep? Yet a little sleep, a little slumber, a little folding of the hands to sleep. So shall thy poverty come as one that travelleth, and thy want as an armed man.' Proverbs, chap. vi.

One more quotation, and I have done. It is from Cowper's Verses supposed to be written by Alexander Selkirk: –

Religion! what treasure untold
Resides in that heavenly word!
More precious than silver and gold,
Or all that this earth can afford.
But the sound of the church-going bell
These valleys and rocks never heard,
Ne'er sighed at the sound of a knell,
Or smiled when a sabbath appeared.

Ye winds, that have made me your sport
Convey to this desolate shore
Some cordial endearing report
Of a land I must visit no more.
My friends, do they now and then send
A wish or a thought after me?
O tell me I yet have a friend,
Though a friend I am never to see.

This passage is quoted as an instance of three different styles of composition. The first four lines are poorly expressed; some Critics would call the language prosaic; the fact is, it would be bad prose, so bad, that it is scarcely worse in metre. The epithet 'church-going' applied to a bell, and that by so chaste a writer as Cowper, is an instance of the strange abuses which Poets have introduced into their language, till they and their Readers take them as matters of course, if they do not single them out expressly as objects of admiration. The two lines 'Ne'er sighed at the sound,' &c., are, in my opinion, an instance of the language of passion wrested from its proper use, and, from the mere circumstance of the composition being in metre, applied upon an occasion that does not justify such violent expressions; and I should condemn the passage, though perhaps few Readers will agree with me, as vicious poetic diction. The last stanza is throughout admirably expressed: it would be equally good whether in prose or verse, except that the Reader has an exquisite pleasure in seeing such natural language so naturally connected with metre. The beauty of this stanza tempts me to conclude with a principle which ought never to be lost sight of, and which has been my chief guide in all I have said, – namely, that in works *of imagination and sentiment*, for of these only have I been treating, in proportion as ideas and feelings are valuable, whether the composition be in prose or in verse, they require and exact one and the same language. Metre is but adventitious to composition, and the phraseology for which that passport is necessary, even where it may be graceful at all, will be little valued by the judicious.

SOURCE: extract from Appendix to the Preface to the Second Edition of *Lyrical Ballads* (1800).

Samuel Taylor Coleridge   (1817)

'Poetic Language and "the language of ordinary men"'

. . . Now I will take the first stanza, on which I have chanced to open, in the *Lyrical Ballads*. It is one the most simple and the least peculiar in its language.

> In distant countries have I been,
> And yet I have not often seen
> A healthy man full grown,
> Weep in the public roads, alone.
> But such a one, on English ground,
> And in the broad highway, I met;
> Along the broad highway he came,
> His cheeks with tears were wet:
> Sturdy he seem'd, though he was sad;
> And in his arms a lamb he had.   [Wordsworth, 'The Last of the Flock']

The words here are doubtless such as are current in all ranks of life; and of course not less so in the hamlet and cottage than in the shop, manufactory, college, or palace. But is this the order, in which the rustic would have placed the words? I am grievously deceived, if the following less compact mode of commencing the same tale be not a far more faithful copy. 'I have been in a many parts, far and near, and I don't know that I ever saw before a man crying by himself in the public road; a

grown man I mean, that was neither sick nor hurt,' &c., &c.
But when I turn to the following stanza in *The Thorn*:

> At all times of the day and night
> This wretched woman thither goes,
> And she is known to every star,
> And every wind that blows:
> And there, beside the thorn, she sits,
> When the blue day-light's in the skies;
> And when the whirlwind's on the hill,
> Or frosty air is keen and still;
> And to herself she cries,
> Oh misery! Oh misery!
> Oh woe is me! Oh misery!

and compare this with the language of ordinary men; or with
that which I can conceive at all likely to proceed, in real life,
from such a narrator, as is supposed in the note to the poem;
compare it either in the succession of the images or of the
sentences; I am reminded of the sublime prayer and hymn of
praise, which Milton, in opposition to an established liturgy,
presents as a fair specimen of common extemporary devotion,
and such as we might expect to hear from every self-inspired
minister of a conventicle! And I reflect with delight, how little
a mere theory, though of his own workmanship, interferes with
the processes of genuine imagination in a man of true poetic
genius. . . .

SOURCE: *Biographia Literaria* (1817), ch. XVIII; modern
edition, George Watson (ed.), 'Everyman's Library'
(London, paperback, 1975).

John Ruskin   (1856)

'The Pathetic Fallacy'

. . . Now, therefore, . . . we may go on at our ease to examine the point in question – namely, the difference between the ordinary, proper, and true appearances of things to us; and the extraordinary or false appearances, when we are under the influence of emotion, or contemplative fancy; false appearances, I say, as being entirely unconnected with any real power or character in the object, and only imputed to it by us. For instance –

> The spendthrift crocus, bursting through the mould
> Naked and shivering, with his cup of gold.

This is very beautiful, and yet very untrue. The crocus is not a spendthrift, but a hardy plant; its yellow is not gold, but saffron. How is it that we enjoy so much the having it put into our heads that it is anything else than a plain crocus?

It is an important question. For, throughout our past reasonings about art, we have always found that nothing could be good, or useful, or ultimately pleasurable, which was untrue. But here is something pleasurable in written poetry which is nevertheless untrue. And what is more, if we think over our favourite poetry, we shall find it full of this kind of fallacy, and that we like it all the more for being so.

It will appear also, on consideration of the matter, that this fallacy is of two principal kinds. Either, as in this case of the crocus, it is the fallacy of wilful fancy, which involves no real expectation that it will be believed; or else it is a fallacy caused by an excited state of the feelings, making us, for the time, more or less irrational. Of the cheating of the fancy we shall have to speak presently; but, in this chapter, I want to examine the nature of the other error, that which the mind admits when

affected strongly by emotion. Thus, for instance, in *Alton Locke*
–

> They rowed her in across the rolling foam –
> The cruel, crawling foam.

The foam is not cruel, neither does it crawl. The state of mind
which attributes to it these characters of a living creature is
one in which the reason is unhinged by grief. All violent
feelings have the same effect. They produce in us a falseness in
all our impressions of external things, which I would generally
characterise as the 'Pathetic Fallacy'.

Now we are in the habit of considering this fallacy as
eminently a character of poetical description, and the temper
of mind in which we allow it as one eminently poetical, because
passionate. But, I believe, if we look well into the matter, that
we shall find the greatest poets do not often admit this kind of
falseness – that it is only the second order of poets who much
delight in it.[1]

Thus, when Dante describes the spirits falling from the bank
of Acheron 'as dead leaves flutter from a bough', he gives the
most perfect image possible of their utter lightness, feebleness,
passiveness, and scattering agony of despair, without,
however, for an instant losing his own clear perception that
these are souls, and *those* are leaves; he makes no confusion of
one with the other. But when Coleridge speaks of

> The one red leaf, the last of its clan,
> That dances as often as dance it can.

he has a morbid, that is to say, a so far false, idea about the
leaf; he fancies a life in it, and will, which there are not;
confuses its powerlessness with choice, its fading death with
merriment, and the wind that shakes it with music. Here,
however, there is some beauty, even in the morbid passage;
but take an instance in Homer and Pope. Without the
knowledge of Ulysses, Elpenor, his youngest follower, has
fallen from an upper chamber in the Circean palace, and has
been left dead, unmissed by his leader, or companions, in the
haste of their departure. They cross the sea to the Cimmerian
land; and Ulysses summons the shades from Tartarus. The

first which appears is that of the lost Elpenor. Ulysses, amazed, and in exactly the spirit of bitter and terrified lightness which is seen in Hamlet,[2] addresses the spirit with the simple, startled words: –

Elpenor! How camest thou under the shadowy darkness? Hast thou come faster on foot than I in my black ship?

Which Pope renders thus: –

O, say, what angry power Elpenor led
To glide in shades, and wander with the dead?
How could thy soul, by realms and seas disjoined,
Outfly the nimble sail, and leave the lagging wind?

I sincerely hope the reader finds no pleasure here, either in the nimbleness of the sail, or the laziness of the wind! . . .

SOURCE: *Modern Painters*, III (1856), Part 4.

NOTES

1. I admit two orders of poets, but no third; and by these two orders I mean the Creative (Shakespeare, Homer, Dante), and Reflective or Perceptive (Wordsworth, Keats, Tennyson). But both of these must be *first*-rate in their range, though their range is different. . . .
2. 'Well said, old mole! can'st work i' the ground so fast?' [*Hamlet*. I v 162].

Matthew Arnold   (1861)

'The Grand Style'

. . . But let us take Scott's poetry at its best; and when it is at its best, it is undoubtedly very good indeed: –

Tunstall lies dead upon the field,
His life-blood stains the spotless shield;

Edmund is down, – my life is reft, –
The Admiral alone is left.
Let Stanley charge with spur of fire, –
With Chester charge, and Lancashire,
Full upon Scotland's central host,
Or victory and England's lost. [*Marmion*, VI 29]

That is, no doubt, as vigorous as possible, as spirited as possible; it is exceedingly fine poetry. And still I say, it is not in the grand manner, and therefore it is not like Homer's poetry. Now, how shall I make him who doubts this feel that I say true; that these lines of Scott are essentially neither in Homer's style nor in the grand style? I may point out to him that the movement of Scott's lines, while it is rapid, is also at the same time what the French call *saccadé*, its rapidity is 'jerky'; whereas Homer's rapidity is flowing rapidity. But this is something external and material; it is but the outward and visible sign of an inward and spiritual diversity. I may discuss what, in the abstract, constitutes the grand style; but that sort of general discussion never much helps our judgment of particular instances. I may say that the presence or absence of the grand style can only be spiritually discerned; and this is true, but to plead this looks like evading the difficulty. My best way is to take eminent specimens of the grand style, and to put them side by side with this of Scott. [Arnold then quotes brief extracts from Homer's *Iliad*, Virgil's *Aeneid*, Dante's *Inferno*, and Milton's *Paradise Lost*, of which only the last is given here.] When Milton says: –

His form had yet not lost
All her original brightness, nor appeared
Less than archangel ruined, and the excess
Of glory obscured, [I 591–4]

that, finally, is in the grand style. Now let any one, after repeating to himself these four passages, repeat again the passage of Scott, and he will perceive that there is something in style which the four first have in common, and which the last is without; and this something is precisely the grand manner. . . .

SOURCE: *On Translating Homer* (1861), Lecture II; reproduced in Sister T. M. Hoctor (ed.), *Arnold's Essays in Criticism* (Chicago, 1969).

Richard Holt Hutton   (1867)

'Internal Evidence for Authorship'

. . . If criticism be not a delusion from the very bottom, this pleasant little story is written by Mr Anthony Trollope. We have no external evidence for saying so, and there is the presumption against it that Mr Trollope's name is worth a great deal in mere money value to the sale of any book. Still, no one who knows this style at all can read three pages of this tale without detecting him as plainly as if he were present in the flesh. Indeed, the present writer has applied what the scientific men call the best test of scientific knowledge, – the power of *prediction* given by the hypothesis that *Nina Balatka* is written by Mr Trollope. The critic said to himself, 'if it is written by Mr Trollope, I shall soon meet with the phrase, "made his way," as applied to walking where there is no physical difficulty or embarrassment, but only a certain moral hesitation as to the end and aim of the walking in question', and behold within a page of the point at which the silent remark was made, came the very phrase in the peculiar sense indicated. And of such test-phrases we could indicate a dozen or so which, as far as we know, are found in Mr Anthony Trollope's stories, and in those alone. . . .

SOURCE: *Spectator* (23 March 1867). Hutton is the probable author of this unsigned review; Trollope's novel had been published anonymously.

A. E. Housman   (1933)

'Augustan Poetic Diction'

[The style of the Augustan poets] could not describe natural objects with sensitive fidelity to nature; it could not express human feelings with a variety and delicacy answering to their own. A thick, stiff, unaccommodating medium was interposed between the writer and his work. And this deadening of language had a consequence beyond its own sphere: its effect worked inward, and deadened perception. That which could no longer be described was no longer noticed.

The features and formation of the style can be studied under a cruel light in Dryden's translations from Chaucer. The Knight's Tale of Palamon and Arcite is not one of Chaucer's most characteristic and successful poems: he is not perfectly at home, as in the Prologue and the tale of Chauntecleer and Pertelote, and his movement is a trifle languid. Dryden's translation shows Dryden in the maturity of his power and accomplishment, and much of it can be honestly and soberly admired. Nor was he insensible to all the peculiar excellence of Chaucer: he had the wit to keep unchanged such lines as 'Up rose the sun and up rose Emily' or 'The slayer of himself yet saw I there'; he understood that neither he nor anyone else could better them. But much too often in a like case he would try to improve, because he thought that he could. He believed, as he says himself, that he was 'turning some of the Canterbury Tales into our language, as it is now refined'; 'the words' he says again 'are given up as a post not to be defended in our poet, because he wanted the modern art of fortifying'; 'in some places' he tells us 'I have added somewhat of my own where I thought my author was deficient, and had not given his thoughts their true lustre, for want of words in the beginning of our language'.

Let us look at the consequences. Chaucer's vivid and memorable line

> The smiler with the knife under the cloke

becomes these three:

> Next stood Hypocrisy, with holy leer,
> Soft smiling and demurely looking down,
> But hid the dagger underneath the gown.

Again:

> Alas, quod he, that day that I was bore.

So Chaucer, for want of words in the beginning of our language. Dryden comes to his assistance and gives his thoughts their true lustre thus:

> Cursed be the day when first I did appear;
> Let it be blotted from the calendar,
> Lest it pollute the month and poison all the year.

Or yet again:

> The queen anon for very womanhead
> Gan for to weep, and so did Emily
> And all the ladies in the company.

If Homer or Dante had the same thing to say, would he wish to say it otherwise? But to Dryden Chaucer wanted the modern art of fortifying, which he thus applies:

> He said; dumb sorrow seized the standers-by.
> The queen, above the rest, by nature good
> (The pattern formed of perfect womanhood)
> For tender pity wept: when she began
> Through the bright quire the infectious virtue ran.
> All dropped their tears, even the contended maid.

Had there not fallen upon England the curse out of Isaiah, 'make the heart of this people fat, and make their ears heavy, and shut their eyes'? That there should ever have existed an obtuseness which could mistake this impure verbiage for a correct and splendid diction is a dreadful thought. More dreadful is the experience of seeing it poured profusely, continually, and with evident exultation, from the pen of a great and deservedly illustrious author. But most dreadful of all is the reflexion that he was himself its principal origin. . . .

SOURCE: *The Name and Nature of Poetry* (Cambridge, 1933), pp. 23-6.

PART TWO
Language and Style: General Considerations

John Spencer & Michael J. Gregory 'Analysing Style' (1964)

A detailed analysis of linguistic features within the text has as one of its aims to cut beneath the generalisations, to get behind the metaphorical labels, of which the literary study of style makes such use. It has always been possible, and indeed valuable, to discuss style in literature by reference simply to the general effect upon all aspects of our sensibilities of which we are conscious when we dwell upon a work of literary art. Such was the course which Middleton Murry set himself in his Oxford Lectures on *The Problem of Style* forty years ago, and he stands in the mainstream of literary stylistics in so doing. But one is then reduced to the use of terms sufficiently all-inclusive and metaphorical to embrace both the response and the organisation of language which is assumed to produce that response. Thus, a 'grand' style presumably offers the reader a sense of grandeur, a 'plain' style a feeling of adequacy without ornament, or a 'baroque' style reminds the reader of a particular kind of architecture. Such shorthand terms are evocative, and fulfil their purpose in so far as they refer to the same response in everyone; and they have therefore considerable use in literary criticism as general categories. They do, however, tend to conflate statements about language with statements about the effects produced by language, and, as Murry recognises in his opening paragraph,[1] they have a habit, like many critical terms, of sliding out of their accustomed place in the framework of literary description if too carefully scrutinised.

A detailed examination of stylistic effects, as opposed to metaphorical labelling, will inevitably lead us to ask the question: If it is said (or if we feel) that this particular style is 'grand', or 'plain', or 'sinewy', in what particular respect does the language provide evidence of grandeur, plainness or sinewy-ness? Are there linguistic correlates to the responses we experience and so label? Such questions are worth asking, and if the answers provide insufficient clues for the analyst to work upon, it is necessary to return again and again to the response, as it develops, to see whether more specific clues cannot be found and a more precise account of it given.

Any linguistic feature may of course possess stylistic significance, but it can be no part of a brief presentation such as this to attempt to list them in detail. To do so would, in fact, produce a catalogue of almost every formal and contextual feature in the language. By way of exemplifying the range, and interrelatedness, of features which may, in different texts, be stylistically significant, therefore, a summary of a few of these will now be made. They have been chosen partly for the illumination they offer of certain stylistic effects and devices often observed but rarely described in detail, and partly also in order to suggest a few lines of inquiry which might bear fruit if pursued in detail in a variety of literary texts.

In the first place, the contribution of grammatical features to stylistic effect has not been much considered or analysed, apart from the generalised, and again often metaphorical, references to the 'rolling' periods or the 'involved' syntax of a writer's language. Concepts of syntactical complexity and simplicity often underly statements of this kind. Linguistic complexity is difficult to measure objectively; but it is possible to describe it in grammatical (and lexical) terms without necessarily quantifying the differences thus exposed. There are, however, not only many degrees of complexity, but many different kinds of complexity; and similarly, a great variety of types of simplicity.

Long sentences do not, of course, necessarily produce a sense of complexity, or what may be termed density of texture. If the clausal relations are paratactic,[2] as they often are in Malory or William Morris, for example, the structure of the prose, being merely additive, is unlikely to give the impression of complexity, other aspects of the text being, so to speak, equal. On the other hand, syntactical hypotaxis is likely to produce the effect of dense, involuted texture, as in much of Henry James's later prose; the rank-shifting which hypotaxis necessarily involves will probably provide, at least in part, a clue to the nature and degree of this complexity. It is clear that the syntactical 'texture' of language may be analysed and tested by grammatical description, provided the grammatical categories and scales which we use enable us to locate different types and degrees of complexity at different places and different 'depths', in terms of the structural patterning which units of differing ranks display.

If, for example, as even a casual reading of many of Sir Thomas Browne's paragraphs suggests, there is carefully contrived syntactical 'balance', it is only by means of a sophisticated grammar that the nature of this balance can be properly discovered and described. In most cases such 'balance', and in Browne even 'palindromic' structure – though he never, it seems, managed a perfect syntactical quincunx[3] in a sentence or paragraph – can be located at one rank, with structural asymmetry at other ranks providing the necessary counterpoise and contrast. Alternatively, balance may be evident at primary structure, but varied by asymmetry at secondary structure. The 'echo' effect of reiteration in dramatic and rhetorical prose is often of this kind, in that it results from syntactical repetition at one rank, with variation at another. This is also characteristic of much poetry and is highly indicative, for example, of the 'set towards the message' in T. S. Eliot's *Ash Wednesday*.

Syntactical effects in poetry not only include complexity and recurrence, but also syntactical ambiguity. Lexical ambiguity has long been recognised in the metaphor, the pun, and other types of imagery, but it is important to observe that ambiguity is not restricted to lexis. The syntax of poetry probably deserves more attention than it has hitherto received, particularly since verse, however 'free', has a double set of units: those of the line and the stanza, and those of syntax. Often one set is used in counterpoint with the other; in the same way that, at the phonological level, metrical patterns are often counterpointed with the rhythms of speech. It is therefore possible for a poet, by juxtaposing grammatical boundaries with those of the metrical line, to make use of syntactical expectancy, followed by syntactical resolution or surprise. In this way alternative syntactical patterns are able to co-exist, thus contributing to the complexity of the verse.

In the drama and the novel, differentiation between dialogue, monologue and narrative, or between speakers, is commonly made by grammatical means, though normally with the aid of lexical and graphological features which support and intensify these differences. Interior monologue in James Joyce's *Ulysses*, for example, is usually marked either by syntactical incompleteness or by full syntax without punctuation. Shakespeare and other dramatists often use incomplete or unresolved syntactical patterns, those major characteristics of spontaneous spoken language, to give the impression of a character intellectualising under strain or in a condition of emotional shock.[4]

A further case which may be instanced where a writer uses grammatical means to produce deliberate effects in his presentation of dialogue is that of Dickens, whose novels richly illuminate the manifold use to which a skilful handling of linguistic differences in speech can be put. An instance of this is his syntactical variation in the presentation of speech in many of his courtroom scenes. A careful examination reveals several different 'degrees' of indirect speech; in some cases it is not possible for the reader to determine whether the author is presenting speech directly, or question and answer conflated, or an indirect summary of the speech of the courtroom, so carefully does Dickens withdraw, partially or wholly, at different points, the grammatical markers of indirect speech.

Syntactical investigations of this kind, if they are intended as a contribution to detailed and explicit statements about style, must of course be matched with, and checked against, the results of careful examinations of the lexis and potential phonology of the texts in question. For grammar can only be a partial contributor to most of these effects. The grammar may display complexity of a particular kind; but lexis may also contribute, and phonological patterning may reinforce syntactical or lexical effects. The intricacy with which collocation and set are managed may, even with a comparatively simple syntax, produce similar, though never precisely the same, effects of involved texture and complexity.

Dylan Thomas's poem *Fern Hill* has a fairly simple syntax, far simpler than that of some of his poems; what complexity the poem has is largely the result of an intricate manipulation of sets and collocations within a relatively complicated metrical form. . . .

SOURCE: extract from Nils Erik Enkvist, John Spencer & Michael J. Gregory, *Linguistics and Style* (London, 1964), pp. 91–6.

NOTES

[Renumbered and reorganised from the original – Ed.]

1. 'It is, I believe, a fairly common experience for those who have been engaged for a good many years in the profession of literary criticism, to slip, almost unconsciously, into a condition of mistrust of all their most familiar and general terms. The critic becomes dissatisfied with the vagueness of his activity, or his art. . . .': *The Problem of Style* (London, 1922), p. 1.

2. [Ed.] *Paratactic*: *parataxis*, in this context, is the placing of clauses in sequence without words to indicate co-ordination or subordination. *Hypotaxis*, referred to in the same paragraph, is the contrary stylistic mode, using words to indicate greater or less degrees of co-ordination or subordination.

3. [Ed.] *Quincunx*: in this stylistic context, a balanced arrangement of five clauses. The term is more generally used in connection with graphic and symbolic art.

4. See, for example, *The Winter's Tale*, I ii 121–7; *Cymbeline*, III ii, 1–17; *Richard III*, V iii 182–93.

George Watson 'Verse and Prose' (1969)

. . . Why do poets write in verse? Coleridge offered a starting-point to an answer when he replied bluntly: 'I write in metre because I am about to use a language different from that of prose.' Metre announces a formality which is about to occur. The pattern in the spoken voice, or the appearance of the poem on the page, warns the listener or the reader against assuming that the utterance he is about to receive is a commonplace one. On the other hand, it is less certain that Coleridge is right when he suggests that the language of verse is necessarily different from that of prose. It may often be so, and there may be cases where it must be so; but to suggest that no other possibility exists is surely to underrate the formality of prose itself. Some poets, such as Wordsworth, employ a prose so formal, even in their private letters, that it is hard to see that the language of their verse needs be formalised in any way – a fact to be borne in mind in considering the preface to *Lyrical Ballads* (1800), where Wordsworth's notion of what constitutes 'the real language of men' is avowedly very different from any ordinary one. A private letter of April 1808, and a poem written at the same time, both describing a dawn walk up Ludgate Hill, may help to confirm the point:

. . . beyond, towering above it, was the huge and majestic form of St Paul's, solemnised by a thin veil of falling snow. I cannot say how much I was affected at this unthought-of sight in such a place, and what a blessing I felt there is in habits of exalted imagination. My sorrow was controlled . . .

and beyond

And high above this winding length of street,
This moveless and unpeopled avenue,
Pure, silent, solemn, beautiful, was seen
The huge majestic temple of St Paul
In awful sequestration, through a veil,
Through its own sacred veil of falling snow.

It remains uncertain whether Wordsworth, in a private letter, would have allowed himself to use such a term as 'awful sequestration'. But if he was prepared in the letter to use phrases as literary as 'solemnised by a thin veil' or 'habits of exalted imagination', then it seems just possible that 'awful sequestration' might have been admissible in his prose as well, and that its presence in the poem alone is an example of an afterthought. At all events, it is not at all clear that the language of the poem is radically more formal than that of the prose. But then the poem is more formal than the letter simply because it is a poem. The fact of metre attracts attention to itself, and demands of the reader that it should be viewed in a more formal way. Even if the language were identical, it would none the less seem different in verse; which is as much as to say that it would in fact be different. It is in this absolute, and perhaps unintended, sense that Coleridge was after all in the right: 'I write in metre because I am about to use a language different from that of prose.' It is just because it is the expectation of our civilisation that the language of verse is different from that of prose that it can, at times, allow itself to be the same.

The formality of verse also makes it the more durable of the two forms: not just in the obvious sense that it makes it easier to get by heart – a fast declining tradition in the present century – but in the more important sense that its formality lends a toughness and a clarity to language. The verse of past ages is often easier to understand than its prose. Shakespeare in the theatre, played before audiences lacking any special instruction in Renaissance English, often seems more lucid in his verse passages than elsewhere. The reasons for this phenomenon are not merely accidental. If Shakespeare, for the most part, prefers verse for his court scenes and prose for the yokels, with the natural consequence that his prose is the more regional, allusive and topical, there are after all good reasons why he should do so: it is not merely a matter of obeying an existing convention. When he violates this natural order, as in *As You Like It*, the inversion is itself a formal property of the play, a rather daring example of the principle of salutary antagonism. What appears to be the intense linguistic naturalism of Hamlet's soliloquy 'To be or not to be', a dramatically convincing example of a reflective intelligence working itself through an untidy argument within the gentle formality of blank verse, is a more subtle example of the same poetic art. There must be many exceptions: but the general tendency of verse is surely to toughen and clarify the texture of language, regardless of whether we choose to learn it by heart or not. Consider a parallel in Donne, which is probably fortuitous. In a letter of September 1608, in characteristic vein, he wrote to a friend:

Therefore I would fain do something; but that I cannot tell what, is no wonder. For to choose, is to do: but to be no part of any body, is to be nothing

Some fifteen years earlier, perhaps, in his third satire he had already written:

Yet strive so, that before age, death's twilight,
Thy soul rest, for none can work in that night.
To will implies delay, therefore now do.
Hard deeds, the body's pains; hard knowledge too
The mind's endeavours reach, and mysteries
Are like the sun – dazzling, yet plain to all eyes.

The two cases are by no means parallel throughout; but at the point where they do run parallel, it is notable that the verse has weathered better than the prose. Formality tends to work as a preservative against time, and verse often endures better than prose. The ordinary language of the past, if it had survived, would surely have dated still more damagingly than the language of literature. . . .

SOURCE: extract from *The Study of Literature* (London, 1969), pp. 53–5.

I. A. Richards 'Sound, Sense, and Interpretation' (1924)

. . . In the reading of poetry the thought due simply to the words, their *sense* it may be called, comes first; but other thoughts are not of less importance. These may be due to the auditory verbal imagery, and we have onomatopoeia,[1] but this is rarely independent of the sense. More important are the further thoughts caused by the sense, the network of interpretation and conjecture which arises therefrom, with its opportunities for aberrations and misunderstanding. Poems, however, differ fundamentally in the extent to which such further interpretation is necessary. The mere sense without any further reflection is very often sufficient thought, in Swinburne, for instance, for the full response –

> There glowing ghosts of flowers
> Draw down, draw nigh;
> And wings of swift spent hours
>   Take flight and fly;
> She sees by formless gleams
> She hears across cold streams
>   Dead mouths of many dreams that sing and sigh.

Little beyond vague thought of the things the words stand for is here required. They do not have to be brought into intelligible connection with one another. On the other hand, Hardy would rarely reach his full effect through sound and sense alone –

> 'Who's in the next room? – who?
>   I seemed to see
> Somebody in the dawning passing through
>   Unknown to me.'
> 'Nay: you saw nought. He passed invisibly.'

Between these and even more extreme cases, every degree of variation in the relative importance of sound, sense, and further interpretation, between form and content in short, can be found. A temptation to which few do not succumb is to suppose that there is some 'proper relation' for these different parts of the experience, so that a poem whose parts are in this relation must thereby be a greater or better poem than another whose parts are differently disposed. This is another instance of the commonest of critical mistakes: the confusion of means with ends, of technique with value. There is no more a 'proper place' for sound or for sense in poetry than there is one and only one 'proper shape' for an animal. A dog is not a defective kind of cat, nor is Swinburne a defective kind of Hardy. But this sort of criticism is extraordinarily prevalent. The objection to Swinburne on the ground of a lack of thought is a popular specimen. . . . .

SOURCE: extract from *Principles of Literary Criticism* (London, 1924), pp. 128–30. (See also pp. 150–1 below.)

NOTE

1. Two kinds of onomatopoeia should be distinguished. In one the sound of the words (actual or imaginal) is like some natural sound (the buzzing of bees, galloping horses, and so forth). In the other it is not like any such sound but such as merely to call up free auditory images of the sounds in question. The second case is by far the more common.

Cleanth Brooks 'The Heresy of Paraphrase' (1947)

. . . Indeed, one may sum up by saying that most of the distempers of criticism come about from yielding to the temptation to take certain remarks which we make *about* the poem – statements about what it says or about what truth it gives or about what formulations it illustrates – for the essential core of the poem itself. As W. M. Urban puts it in his *Language and Reality*: 'The general principle of the inseparability of intuition and expression holds with special force for the aesthetic intuition. Here it means that form and content, or content and medium, are inseparable. The artist does not first intuit his object and then find the appropriate medium. It is rather in and through his medium that he intuits the object.' So much for the process of composition. As for the critical process: 'To pass from the intuitable to the nonintuitable is to negate the function and meaning of the symbol.' For it 'is precisely because the more universal and ideal relations cannot be adequately expressed directly that they are indirectly egressed by means of the more intuitible'. The most obvious examples of such error (and for that reason those which are really least dangerous) are those theories which frankly treat the poem as propaganda. The most subtle (and the most stubbornly rooted in the ambiguities of language) are those which, beginning with the 'paraphrasable' elements of the poem, refer the other elements of the poem finally to some role subordinate to the paraphrasable elements. (The relation between all the elements must surely be an organic one – there can be no question about that. There is, however, a very serious question as to whether the paraphrasable elements have primacy.)

[Yvor] Winters's position will furnish perhaps the most respectable example of the paraphrastic heresy. He assigns primacy to the 'rational meaning' of the poem. 'The relationship, in the poem, between rational statement and feeling', he remarks in his latest book,[1] 'is thus seen to be that of motive to emotion.' He goes on to illustrate his point by a brief and excellent analysis of the following lines from Browning:

> So wore night; the East was gray,
>   White the broad-faced hemlock flowers. . . .

'The verb *wore*', he continues, 'means literally that the night passed, but it carries with it connotations of exhaustion and attrition which belong to the condition of the protagonist; and grayness is a colour which we associate with such a condition. If we change the phrase to read: ''Thus night passed'', we shall have the same rational meaning, and a metre quite as respectable, but no trace of the power of the line: the connotation of *wore* will be lost, and the connotation of *gray* will remain in a state of ineffective potentiality.'

But the word *wore* does not mean *literally* 'that the night passed'; it means literally 'that the night *wore*' – whatever *wore* may mean, and, as Winters's own admirable analysis indicates, *wore* 'means', whether *rationally* or *irrationally*, a great deal. Furthermore, 'So wore night' and 'Thus night passed' can be said to have 'the same rational meaning' only if we equate 'rational meaning' with the meaning of a loose paraphrase. And can a loose paraphrase be said to be the 'motive to emotion'? Can it be said to 'generate' the feelings in question? (Or, would Mr Winters not have us equate 'rational statement' and 'rational meaning'?)

Much more is at stake here than any quibble. In view of the store which Winters sets by rationality and of his penchant for poems which make their evaluations overtly, and in view of this frequent blindness to those poems which do not – in view of these considerations, it is important to see that what 'So wore night' and 'Thus night passed' have in common as their 'rational meaning' is not the 'rational meaning' of each but the lowest common denominator of both. To refer the structure of the poem to what is finally a paraphrase of the poem is to refer it to something outside the poem.

To repeat, most of our difficulties in criticism are rooted in the heresy of paraphrase. If we allow ourselves to be misled by it, we distort the relation of the poem to its 'truth', we raise the problem of belief in a vicious and crippling form, we split the poem between its 'form' and its 'content' – we bring the statement to be conveyed into an unreal competition with science or philosophy or theology. In short, we put our questions about the poem in a form calculated to produce the battles of the last twenty-five years over the 'use of poetry'.[2]

If we allow ourselves to be misled by the heresy of paraphrase, we run the risk of doing even more violence to the internal order of the poem itself. By taking the paraphrase as our point of stance, we misconceive the function of metaphor and metre. We demand logical coherences where they are sometimes irrelevant, and we fail frequently to see imaginative coherences on levels where they are highly relevant. . . .

SOURCE: extract from *The Well-Wrought Urn: Studies in the Structure of Poetry* (New York, 1947; London, 1949), pp. 182–5.

NOTES

[Reorganised and renumbered from the original – Ed.]

1. [Ed.] Yvor Winters. *In Defense of Reason* (Denver, Col., 1947; rev. edn, 1960).
2. I do not, of course, intend to minimise the fact that some of these battles have been highly profitable, or to imply that the foregoing paragraphs could have been written except for the illumination shed by the discussions of the last twenty-five years.

T. S. Eliot   'Meaning and Music' (1942)

. . . It may appear strange, that when I profess to be talking about the 'music' of poetry, I put such emphasis upon conversation. But I would remind you, first, that the music of poetry is not something which exists apart from the meaning. Otherwise, we could have poetry of great musical beauty which made no sense, and I have never come across such poetry. The apparent exceptions only show a difference of degree: there are poems in which we are moved by the music and take the sense for granted, just as there are poems in which we attend to the sense and are moved by the music without noticing it. Take an apparently extreme example – the nonsense verse of Edward Lear. His non-sense is not vacuity of sense: it is a parody of sense, and that is the sense of it. *The Jumblies* is a poem of adventure, and of nostalgia for the romance of foreign voyage and exploration; *The Yongy-Bongy Bo* and *The Dong with a Luminous Nose* are poems of unrequited passion – 'blues' in fact. We enjoy the music, which is of a high order, and we enjoy the feeling of irresponsibility towards the sense. Or take a poem of another type, the *Blue Closet* of William Morris. It is a delightful poem, though I cannot explain what it means and I doubt whether the author could have explained it. It has an effect somewhat like that of a rune or charm, but runes and charms are very practical formulae designed to produce definite results, such as getting a cow out of a bog. But its obvious intention (and I think the author succeeds) is to produce the effect of a dream. It is not necessary, in order to enjoy the poem, to know what the dream means; but human beings have an unshakeable belief that dreams mean something: they used to believe – and many still believe – that dreams disclose the secrets of the future; the orthodox modern faith is that they reveal the secrets – or at least the more horrid secrets – of the past. It is a commonplace to observe that the meaning of a poem may wholly escape paraphrase. It is not quite so commonplace to observe that the meaning of a poem may be something larger than its author's conscious purpose, and something remote from its origins. One of the more obscure of modern poets was the French writer Stéphane Mallarmé, of whom the French sometimes say that his language is so peculiar that it can be understood only by foreigners. The late Roger Fry, and his friend Charles Mauron, published an English translation with notes to unriddle the meanings: when I learn that a difficult sonnet was inspired by seeing a painting on the ceiling reflected on the polished top of a table, or by seeing the light reflected from the foam on a glass of beer, I can only say that this may be a correct embryology, but it is not the meaning. If we are moved by a poem, it has meant something, perhaps something important, to us; if we are not moved, then it is, as poetry, meaningless. We can be deeply stirred by hearing the recitation of a poem in a language of which we understand no word; but if we are then told that the poem is gibberish and has no meaning, we shall consider that we have been deluded – this was no poem, it was merely an imitation of instrumental music. If, as we are aware, only a part of the meaning can be conveyed by paraphrase, that is because the poet is occupied with frontiers of consciousness beyond which words fail, though meanings still exist. A poem may appear to mean very different things to different readers, and all of these meanings may be different from what the author thought he meant. For instance, the author may have been writing some peculiar personal experience, which he saw quite unrelated to anything outside; yet for the reader the poem may become the expression of a general situation, as well as of some private experience of his own. The reader's interpretation may differ from the author's and be equally valid – it may even be better. There may be much more in a poem than the author was aware of. The different interpretations may all be partial formulations of one thing; the ambiguities may be due to the fact that the poem means more, not less, than ordinary speech can communicate.

So, while poetry attempts to convey something beyond what can be conveyed in prose rhythms, it remains, all the same, one person talking to another; and this is just as true if you sing it, for singing is another way of talking. The immediacy of poetry to conversation is not a matter on which we can lay down exact laws. Every revolution in poetry is apt to be, and sometimes to announce itself to be, a return to common speech. That is the revolution which Wordsworth announced in his prefaces, and he was right: but the same revolution had been carried out a century before by Oldham, Waller, Denham and Dryden; and the same revolution was due again something over a century later. The followers of a revolution develop the new poetic idiom in one direction or another; they polish or perfect it; meanwhile the spoken language goes on changing, and the poetic idiom goes out of date. Perhaps we do not realise how natural the speech of Dryden must have sounded to the most sensitive of his contemporaries. No poetry, of course, is ever exactly the same speech that the poet talks and hears: but it has to be in such a relation to the speech of his time that the listener or reader can say 'that is how I should talk if I could talk poetry'. This is the reason why the best contemporary poetry can give us a feeling of excitement and a sense of fulfilment different from any sentiment aroused by even very much greater poetry of a past age.

The music of poetry, then, must be a music latent in the common speech of its time. And that means also that it must be latent in the common speech of the poet's *place*. It would not be to my present purpose to inveigh against the ubiquity of standardised, or 'BBC' English. If we all came to talk alike there would no longer be any point in our not writing alike: but until that time comes – and I hope it may be long postponed – it is the poet's business to use the speech which he finds about him, that with which he is most familiar. I shall always remember the impression of W. B. Yeats reading poetry aloud. To hear him read his own works was to be made to recognise how much the Irish way of speech is needed to bring out the beauties of Irish poetry: to hear Yeats reading William Blake was an experience of a different kind, more astonishing than satisfying. Of course, we do not want the poet merely to reproduce exactly the conversational idiom of himself, his family, his friends and his particular district: but what he finds there is the material out of which he must make his poetry. He must, like the sculptor, be faithful to the material in which he works; it is out of sounds that he has heard that he must make his melody and harmony.

It would be a mistake, however, to assume that all poetry ought to be melodious, or that melody is more than one of the components of the music of words. Some poetry is meant to be sung; most poetry, in modern times, is meant to be spoken – and there are many other things to be spoken of besides the murmur of innumerable bees or the moan of doves in immemorial elms. Dissonance, even cacophony, has its place: just as, in a poem of any length, there must be transitions between passages of greater and less intensity, to give a rhythm of fluctuating emotion essential to the musical structure of the whole; and the passages of less intensity will be, in relation to the level on which the total poem operates, prosaic – so that, in the sense implied by that context, it may be said that no poet can write a poem of amplitude unless he is a master of the prosaic.[1]

What matters, in short, is the whole poem: and if the whole

poem need not be, and often should not be, wholly melodious, it follows that a poem is not made only out of 'beautiful words'. I doubt whether, from the point of view of *sound* alone, any word is more or less beautiful than another – within its own language, for the question whether some languages are not more beautiful than others is quite another question. The ugly words are the words not fitted for the company in which they find themselves; there are words which are ugly because of rawness or because of antiquation; there are words which are ugly because of foreignness or ill-breeding (e.g. *television*): but I do not believe that any word well-established in its own language is either beautiful or ugly. The music of a word is, so to speak, at a point of intersection: it arises from its relation first to the words immediately preceding and following it, and indefinitely to the rest of its context; and from another relation, that of its immediate meaning in that context to all the other meanings which it has had in other contexts, to its greater or less wealth of association. Not all words, obviously, are equally rich and well-connected: it is part of the business of the poet to dispose the richer among the poorer, at the right points, and we cannot afford to load a poem too heavily with the former – for it is only at certain moments that a word can be made to insinuate the whole history of a language and a civilisation. This is an 'allusiveness' which is not the fashion or eccentricity of a peculiar type of poetry; but an allusiveness which is in the nature of words, and which is equally the concern of every kind of poet. My purpose here is to insist that a 'musical poem' is a poem which has a musical pattern of sound and a musical pattern of the secondary meanings of the words which compose it, and that these two patterns are indissoluble and one. And if you object that it is only the pure sound, apart from the sense, to which the adjective 'musical' can be rightly applied, I can only reaffirm my previous assertion that the sound of a poem is as much an abstraction from the poem as is the sense. . . .

SOURCE: extract from 'The Music of Poetry', originally given as a lecture in 1942 and included in *On Poetry and Poets* (London, 1957), pp. 29–33.

NOTE

1. This is the complementary doctrine to that of the 'touchstone' line or passage of Matthew Arnold: this test of the greatness of a poet is the way he writes his less intense, but structurally vital matter.

George Rylands   'Metre and Sound in Poetry'   (1928)

. . . Metre has certain effects upon language. First of all it creates boundaries and limits, which are very useful. The poet may override them, when he so desires: but even in the blank verse of, say, Shirley, there remains the visual division, and the actor pauses imperceptibly at the end of the line. One advantage of these boundaries is that they enable the changes of style, noticed above, changes which are unnatural and almost impossible from sentence to sentence in prose. Housman's *Last Poems* will give an example of a division, intensifying the language by contrast:

> The fairies break their dances,
>   And leave the printed lawn,
> And up from India glances
>   The silver sail of dawn.
>
> The candles burn their sockets,
>   The blinds let through the day,
> The young man feels his pockets
>   And wonders what's to pay.

The Italian sonnet form with the break between the octave and sestet often occasions similar effects, and the final clinching couplet of the Shakespearean sonnet, not to mention Pope's exploitation of the heroic couplet, show the possibilities of metrical boundaries.

Then again in a line which is separated off, a line in which the words are numbered and must be fitted as the figures are fitted into a pediment, it is possible to achieve a harmony and interdependence of words, too subtle for the ear to catch or the mind to grasp in the swifter and more continuous reading of prose. The invisible fetters with which the poet binds his words together may be alliterative. Let us take another of the *Last Poems*:

	On acres of the seeded grasses	s ss s
b n	The changing burnish heaves;	ch sh s
m m n	Or marshalled under moons of harvest	sh s st
n	Stand still all night the sheaves;	st st t sh
b n w	Or beeches strip in storms for winter	ch st st t
n w	And stain the wind with leaves.	st s

The play is mainly upon *sh ch st*. If it is objected that Housman is an exceptionally careful artist, one need only refer the unbeliever to an article by Stevenson in the *Contemporary Review* (1885), analysing a passage in *Troilus and Cressida*, as follows:

But in the wind and tempest of her frown,	w p v f st ow
Distinction with a loud and powerful fan,	w p f st ow l
Puffing at all, winnows the light away;	w p f l
And what hath mass and matter by itself	w f h m
Lies rich in virtue and unmingled.	v l m

[A. W.] Verrall, as I have heard, used to point out Shakespeare's artfulness in the rhetorical tricks of Brutus.

Who is here so *base* that would be a *bondman*? If any, speak; for him have I offended. Who is here so *rude* that would not be a *Roman*? If any, speak; for him have I offended. Who is here so *vile* that will not *love* his country? If any, speak; for him have I offended.

The blunt alliterations are followed by the inversion of *love* and *vile*. The art of poetry, according to a modern poet, consists in knowing exactly how to manipulate the letter S. The best example of this that I know is to be found in *Comus*.

th d t	A *thousand* fan*ta*sies	s s s
b th t	Begin *to thr*ong in*to* my memory	
b d d	Of calling *shapes* and beck'ning *shadows d*ire,	sh s sh s
d t th b	And airy *to*ngues *that* sylla*b*le men's names	s s s s
d d t d	On *Sand*s, and *Shoar*s, and *Desert* Wildernesses.	s s sh sss

The Ss gather in number but are leavened with hard letters: L, M and N play a part also. The last line has two strong pauses which draw out the eight S sounds like a wind whistling over waste spaces.

Sometimes one letter appears and reappears, threading a poem or paragraph. Thus the less common letter V in Marvell's *Coy Mistress*. The first suggestion comes in three consecutive lines: *conversion, vegetable, vaster*, then *deserve*; then in the centre panel a combination with F. *Before, vast, found, vault; preserved virginity; grave, fine, private*. This panel of twelve lines is, indeed, subtle and faultless. The sixth line runs on and carries one over from the first into the second half: the beginning and the close are marked by a strong couplet. The second and fourth couplets have unstressed rhymes which keep up the speed.

Tennyson is a gentle juggler with words. He experiments with syllables:

> Myriads of rivulets hurrying through the lawn,

with letters:

> Between the loud stream and the trembling stars,

(Here the consonants repeat and the vowels are varied, a common effect; the caesura is strong and the monosyllable *stream* robs *and* of its natural stress.)
with emphases:

> Coldly thy rosy shadows bathe me, cold
> Are all thy lights, and cold my wrinkled feet.

This last device, epanaphora, is frequent in Tennyson and not rare in Milton. Metre enables the poet to underline a word as it were: all shades of emphasis are possible. Contrast, for instance, on the word *dear*:

> My dear and only love, I pray.
> > MONTROSE
> I could not love thee, Dear, so much.
> > LOVELACE
> If yet I have not all thy love,
> Dear, I shall never have it all.
> > DONNE
> A terrible childbed hast thou had, my dear.
> > SHAKESPEARE

SOURCE: extract from *Words and Poetry* (London, 1928), pp. 38–41.

Winifred Nowottny (1962)   'Poetic Syntax'

. . . Of all the ·elements necessary to make an utterance meaningful, the most powerful is syntax, controlling as it does the order in which impressions are received and conveying the mental relations 'behind' sequences of words. And since we naturally tend – except when checked by a difficulty – to take in without effort the relations conveyed by syntax, its operation as a cause of poetical pleasure is often the last cause we recognise, if indeed we recognise it at all. The result is that syntax is important to poet and to critic because it produces strong effects by stealth; these remain 'inexplicable' so long as the power of syntax goes undetected. For instance: many people have observed the sublime effect of the passage (Genesis, i 3), 'And God said, Let there be light: and there was light', but it was left to Spitzer[1] to trace the sublime effect to its cause – in the fact that the syntax in which the fulfilment of God's command is described is as close as possible to the syntax of the command itself. (In the original Hebrew, as Spitzer points out, the parallelism of command and fulfilment is even closer: *jĕhī aur vajĕhī aur*.) In this instance the cause of those strong effects which the reader naturally perceives but cannot explain to himself lies in the fact that because of the compelling syntactical relations in each passage, the reader's mind receives not only the information the passage may be said to communicate but also and at the same time the significance of the information. The Genesis passage informs us of the fact that, and of the manner in which, God created light; the exact form in which this information is conveyed compels us to regard it as meaning, further, that what God willed was forthwith brought to pass exactly according to His word as the consequence of that word; these significances proceed from the relations, apprehended in a flash by the reader's mind, between the parts of the command (and their organisation) and the parts of the fulfilment (and their organisation).

Some such apprehension in a flash is a mental event the reader cannot avoid experiencing, since as a user of language he is conditioned to attach meaning to syntactical relations without conscious effort; the meaning of an utterance as a whole does not reach him at all unless it reaches him already arranged into the set of relations syntax imposes on the words the utterance contains. Consequently syntax, however little it is noted by the reader, is the groundwork of the poet's art. Often it supports a poetic edifice elaborated by many other poetic means and the reader is content to believe that these other means are the cause of his pleasure, but when a passage relies chiefly on its especially compelling and artful syntax to make its effect, the reader and the critic who never expect syntax to be more than 'a harmless, necessary drudge' holding open the door while the pageantry of words sweeps through, will be at a loss to understand why the passage affects them as it does and at a loss to do critical justice to its art.

There is more at stake than the critic's chances of being able to make less inexplicable those passages whose art is primarily syntactical. In many cases there will prove to be a fruitful interplay between syntactical relations and other formal systems – as for instance the rhyme-scheme. This is so in Pope's well-known lines (*Pastorals*, II, 73–6):

> Where-e'er you walk, cool gales shall fan the glade,
> Trees, where you sit, shall crowd into a shade,
> Where-e'er you tread, the blushing flow'rs shall rise,
> And all things flourish where you turn your eyes.

Here the management of the rhymes cannot be fully appreciated unless one relates them to the flow and ebb of expectations set up by skilful management of syntax. The first of these lines balances about the pause after 'walk'; before the pause comes the human action, after it the effect on Nature.

The second line repeats this strong pause but introduces a syntactical variation: 'Trees' (which corresponds syntactically to 'cool glades') is put first in the line and is further emphasised by an irregular strong stress; 'where you sit', which follows, makes us expect that this second line will in some way repeat the pattern of the first. So we expect to be told what the trees will do, and because we are made to wait for the verb, this expectation becomes a felt desire for the completion of the pattern – a desire which is then not only satisfied but amply satisfied when the pattern expands ('shall crowd into') and then returns to rest when 'a shade' brings this line into correspondence with 'the glade' in the line before. The opening of the third line reaffirms the formula of the opening of the first, with the words 'Where-e'er you tread', and one interprets this as a recapitulation of theme that must lead to a further variation. When that variation does come ('the blushing flow'rs'), it provides at the same time a dilation of that element of the pattern which had contracted in the previous line (where 'Trees' had replaced 'cool glades'). This third line does not, like the second, return to rest, for it ends with 'shall rise'; here there is no counterpart to 'the glade', 'a shade'. The fourth line is a complex and surprising resolution of this crisis in the pattern. First it sums into a satisfactory climax the sequence 'gales' – 'Trees' – 'flowers' with the phrase 'And all things'. The following verb, however, still leaves unsatisfied our wish for a counterpart to 'glade' and 'shade'. Delayed thus, the urge to fulfilment is stronger, and to it is added the pressure of expectation of a counterpart to 'Where[-e'er] you walk/sit/tread'. Suddenly both demands are fulfilled simultaneously: the latter in 'where you turn your eyes', the former in the fact that *this* phrase now provides the transitive verb and the object, so that 'you turn your eyes' is a return to the syntactical pattern of the second half of the first line ('cool gales shall fan the glade': subject – verb – object) and at the same time it brings the quatrain to an end by neatly reversing the initial disposition of the two major parts of the overall pattern:

Where-e'er you walk,   cool gales shall fan the glade,

.   .   .   . ⟋. .   .   .   .
.   .   .   ⟍.   .   .   .

And all things flourish   where you turn your eyes.

It is only with respect to these manipulations of expectancy that one can estimate the art shown in the rhymes. The rhyme 'glade'/'shade' is unsurprising (it rhymes noun with noun, the nouns naming comparable things) and this is suitable for this point in the pattern (for here the second line returns to rest); in contrast, the rhyme 'rise'/'eyes' more surprisingly rhymes a verb with a noun, and the verb occupies a position on the crest of rhyme and syntax that one can estimate the fitness of the position in the pattern that it resolves all the remaining expectations of the poem in a simultaneous fulfilment. Moreover it is only with respect to all this activity with patterns of rhyme and syntax that one can estimate the fitness of the diction for its purposes. Such a diction, worn smooth with use, has no anfractuosities[2] to distract us from the witty evolution of the patterns I have discussed; its unruffled surface is almost a necessary condition of our being set at ease to follow the patterns moving beneath it with such agile assurance.

It should be clear from this last example that elements as diverse as syntax, rhyme and diction usually have to be considered together because of their interpenetration of one another. . . .

SOURCE: extract from *The Language Poets Use* (London, 1962), pp. 9–12.

NOTES

[Reorganised from the original – Ed.]

1. Leo Spitzer, 'Language of Poetry', in Ruth Nanda Anshen (ed.), *Language: An Enquiry into Its Meaning and Function*, Science of Culture Series, VIII (New York, 1957), p. 210.
2. [Ed.] *Anfractuosity*: intricacy, winding in and out.

Jonathan Culler   'On Parody' (1975)

. . . When a text cites or parodies the conventions of a genre one interprets it by moving to another level of interpretation where both terms of the opposition can be held together by the theme of literature itself. But the text which parodies a particular work requires a somewhat different mode of reading. Though two different orders must be held together in the mind – the order of the original and the point of view which undermines the original – this does not generally lead to synthesis and to naturalisation at another level but rather to an exploration of the difference and resemblance. . . . In calling something a parody we are specifying how it should be read, freeing ourselves from the demands of poetic seriousness, and making the curious features of the parody intelligible. The amazing alliteration, the thrusting anapestic rhythm, and the absence of content in Swinburne's self-parody, 'Nephelidia', are immediately recuperated and given significance when we read it as parody: we read them as imitations and exaggerations of features of the original.

If it is to avoid burlesque, parody must capture something of the spirit of the original as well as imitate its formal devices and produce through slight variation – usually of lexical items – a distance between the *vraisemblance* of the original and its own. 'I see how this poem works; look at how easy it is to show up the sententiousness of this poem; its effects are imitable and hence artificial; its achievement is fragile and depends on conventions of reading being taken seriously.' That is essentially the spirit of parody. Generally it invites one to a more literal reading, establishing a contrast between the naturalisation required for appreciation of the original and the more literal interpretive process appropriate to the parody. Part of this effect is no doubt due to the fact that parody is an imitation and that by making its model explicit it implicitly denies that it is to be read as a serious statement of feelings about real problems or situations, thus freeing us from one type of *vraisemblance* used to enforce metaphorical readings of poems. Henry Reed's 'Chard Whitlow', one of the best parodies of Eliot, uses lines which, in Eliot, would receive proper metaphorical naturalisation but places them in a context which leads us to read them differently:

> As we get older we do not get any younger.
> Seasons return, and today I am fifty-five,
> And this time last year I was fifty-four,
> And this time next year I shall be sixty-two.
> And I cannot say I should like (to speak for myself)
> To see my time over again – if you can call it time:
> Fidgeting uneasily under the draughty stair,
> Or counting sleepless nights in the crowded tube.

The series of ages enforces a literal reading of the first line, preventing tautology from finding its function at another level, as seems to happen in *Four Quartets* (As we grow older/The world becomes stranger). And thus 'time' in 'if you can call it time' is only allowed to hover on the edge of metaphysical exploration before teetering back into comic bathos. In other contexts the last two lines might function as powerful non-empirical images, but here we are stopped by the absurdity of the empirical images – of these ways of actually passing one's time. And the brilliant line, 'The wind within a wind unable to speak for wind', which parodies the beginning of section five of *Ash Wednesday* (Still is the unspoken word, the Word unheard,/The Word without a word, the Word within/The world and for the world), reinforces, by the substitution of 'wind', the suggestion of pomposity which serves as the integrating function of the parody. Whereas the surface pomposities of *Four Quartets* (And what you own is what you do not own/And where you are is where you are not) are located and tempered by immediate shifts into another mode which can be read as indirect comment (The wounded surgeon plies the steel/That questions the distempered part), the *vraisemblance* of the parody insists on a literal reading which displays the distance between the 'natural' interpretation and what is required by Eliot's verse when it is taken seriously. . . .

SOURCE: extract from *Structuralist Poetics: Structuralism, Linguistics and the Study of Literature* (London, 1975), pp. 152–5.

David Lodge 'Repetition in the Novel' (1966)

. . . in my own view, the perception of repetition is the first step towards offering an account of the way language works in extended literary texts, such as novels. The use of such evidence in literary criticism is, however, open to certain objections which I should like to try and anticipate by the following propositions.

Firstly, the significance of repetition in a given text is not conditional on its being a deliberate and conscious device on the author's part.

It is not quite sufficient to defend this proposition by a simple gesture towards the intentional fallacy. While acknowledging that criticism deals only with intentions discoverable in the work itself, we must also recognise that, on the linguistic level, some works declare their intentions more overtly than others, and that this must affect the nature of the work and our response to it. The key-words of Joseph Conrad's novels and stories, for instance – *darkness* in *Heart of Darkness*, *youth* in *Youth*, *silver* and *material interests* in *Nostromo*, for example – are kept reverberating in our ears by conscious contrivance. Conrad has in fact given us a clue to his method through the fictitious narrator of *Under Western Eyes*:

The task is not in truth the writing in the narrative form a précis of a strange human document, but the rendering – I perceive it now clearly – of the moral conditions ruling over a large portion of the earth's surface [i.e., Russia]; conditions not easily to be understood, much less discovered in the limits of a story, till some keyword is found; a word that could stand at the back of all the words covering the pages, a word which, if not truth itself, may perchance hold truth enough to help the moral discovery which should be the object of every tale.[1]

But with another kind of writer – Charlotte Brontë for example – one suspects that the reiteration of certain symbols or motifs was an intuitive or compulsive process driven by the emotional pressures behind the writing. This is not to suggest that Charlotte Brontë poured out her work in a kind of inspired trance. Mrs Gaskell tells us [in *The Life of Charlotte Brontë*] that

One set of words was the truthful mirror of her thoughts; no others, however apparently identical in meaning, would do. . . . She would wait patiently, searching for the right term, until it presented itself to her. It might be provincial, it might be derived from the Latin; so that it accurately represented her idea, she did not mind whence it came. . . . She never wrote down a sentence until she deeply understood what she wanted to say, had deliberately chosen the words, and had arranged them in their right order

But Charlotte Brontë herself, on one occasion, gave an account of the creative process which has a different emphasis from Mrs Gaskell's, an emphasis which is more in accord with the quality of her writing as we experience it:

When authors write best, or, at least, when they write most fluently, an influence wakens in them, which becomes their master – which will have its own way – putting out of view all behests but its own, dictating certain words, and insisting on their being used, whether vehement or measured in their nature . . . [Letter to G. H. Lewes, 18 January 1848.]

We might speculate that while each individual reference to, say, *fire*, in *Jane Eyre*, was formulated in a way determined by conscious artistic effort, Charlotte Brontë's persistent *return* to this word and associated words, which contributes significantly to its unity and identity, was not a consciously executed manoeuvre in the manner of Conrad. My point is merely that in perceiving and pointing out significant patterns of repetition, we do not need to be encouraged by the approving nods of the author over our shoulders.

Secondly, the significance of repetition in a given text is not conditional on its being consciously and spontaneously recognised by a majority of intelligent readers.

A failure to appreciate this point accounts, I believe, for a good deal of the resistance offered to the kind of criticism I have been recommending. Confronted with the demonstration of a certain pattern of repetition, which they have not themselves noticed, in a familiar text, many readers feel that their own reading, or way of reading, is being radically challenged. This is not necessarily the case. If both demonstration and reading are sound, the former will consolidate and enrich the latter. Criticism of the kind I propose is an analytic procedure applied to a synthetic process – the total, accumulative effect of a work of art. Most 'lay readers', and many literary critics, choose to articulate their response to a literary text by an impressionistic description of this synthesis – a valid but chancy procedure. But any significant pattern of repetition will have contributed to this synthesis.[2]

Thirdly, the significance of repetition is not to be determined statistically.

The most frequently recurring word in a given text is not necessarily the most significant word. If it were, computers could perform the initial critical task for us. Only the critical intelligence can make the continual reference between part and whole which permits discrimination between degrees of significance in the recurring linguistic elements of a literary text.

Once, however, a particular iterative feature of the text has been isolated as being especially useful to the critical understanding of the whole, its merely numerical frequency of occurrence will have a certain interest and relevance.[3]

Fourthly, repetition of any kind does not, in itself, confer value on literary texts.

To use *dark* and *darkness* and associated words as often as Conrad uses them in *Heart of Darkness* is not a formula for writing a great work of literature. Yet the insistent recurrence of this verbal cluster has much to do with the power of Conrad's story. The effectiveness of the story subsists in the relationships between the overall structural scheme and the rich textural particularity of local detail. In following the structural theme of *darkness* through the texture of the story, observing each occurrence in its context, criticism can offer some account of that sense of unity in multiplicity which works like *Heart of Darkness* impart to their readers.[4]

To take a different kind of case: Professor David Daiches has called attention to the function of certain recurrent verbal features of Virginia Woolf's novels. (1) Her use of the third person pronoun, *one* ('it was not her one hated, but the idea of her'), as a way of indicating a certain agreement on the part of the writer with a character's thoughts.[5] (2) Her use of *for* to link different stages of association in a character's stream of consciousness – 'To dance, to ride, she had adored all that. (New para.) For they might be parted for hundreds of years, she and Peter' – *for* being 'a word which does not indicate a strict logical sequence . . . but does suggest a relationship which is at least half-logical'.[6] (3) Her persistent use of present participles of action ('Such fools, we are, she thought, crossing Victoria Street') 'to allow the author to remind the reader of the character's position, without interrupting the thought stream'.[7]

There is no doubt that these are significant expressive features of Virginia Woolf's work, or that they have the effects described by Daiches. But one could go further and make the following points: (1) The use of the pronoun *one* is a characteristic upper-middle-class speech habit which, while it appears to withdraw modestly from crude assertion, slyly invokes authority from some undefined community of feeling and prejudice, into which it seeks to draw the auditor. Has Virginia Woolf entirely resolved her own attitude to characters like Mrs Dalloway, and is she entirely open about the degree of indulgence she expects the reader to extend to them? (2) The use of *for* to suggest logical connection where none exists might reveal a certain timidity in exploring the flow of consciousness and a disposition to simplify its workings. (3) The verb-participle construction establishes a divorce between cerebration and physical action which is not as normative as Virginia Woolf's fiction implies. We do not always think of eternity while serving potatoes; sometimes we just think of serving potatoes. Virginia Woolf's characters never do.

In other words, the devices brought forward by Daiches to illustrate Virginia Woolf's expressive use of language, while they certainly help to explain how her presentation of experience gets its special character, might be used as evidence for alleging certain important limitations in her art. In this event, the very frequency of occurrence which makes these devices significant would be seen as damaging, contributing to an overall effect of monotonous sameness in the presentation of consciousnesses whose unique constitutions should be reflected in the language (as for instance in the comparable fiction of Joyce). This would be a possible line of argument,[8] and serves to show that the same set of linguistic facts can be used to reach quite opposite critical conclusions.

Iterative patterns are thus never, in themselves, explanations of meaning or value. They may, or may not, offer useful and illuminating ways of accounting for meaning and value in literary texts. Whether they do so, and how they do so, will depend entirely upon the critical use that is made of them. . . .

SOURCE: extract from *Language of Fiction* (London, 1966), pp. 82–7.

NOTES

[Reorganised and renumbered from the original – Ed.]

1. Conrad, *Under Western Eyes* (1911), I iii. In *Under Western Eyes* the key-word is cynicism – a somewhat surprising one, which no doubt explains why Conrad calls attention to it so explicitly.

2. I recently encountered an interesting illustration of this in Lord David Cecil's chapter on Charlotte Brontë in *Early Victorian Novelists*. I show, in Part Two Chapter II [of *Language of Fiction* – Ed.], the prominence of references, literal and metaphorical, to *fire* in *Jane Eyre*. Lord David approaches Charlotte Brontë's work in a very different way, and I disagree with many of his judgments, but I was struck by the fact that, without explicit quotation or allusion to the text, he persistently uses fire-imagery to convey his impressions. E.g.:

'For they [the characters] come to us through the transfiguring medium of Charlotte Brontë's volcanic imagination. Lit by its lurid glare, these prosaic schools and parsonages stand out huge, secret, momentous. These commonplace drawing-rooms glow with a strange brightness,

these plain corridors are sinister with stirring shadows.' (Penguin edn (1948), p. 103.)
'Their loves and hates and ambitions are alike fiery and insatiable.' (Ibid., p. 104.)
'Childish naiveté, rigid Puritanism, fiery passion. . . .' (Ibid., p. 105.)
'her ingenuousness . . . disinfects her imagination; blows away the smoke and sulphur which its ardent heat might be expected to generate, so that its flame blows pure and clear.' (Ibid., p. 105.)
'the fire of her personality. . . .' (Ibid., p. 110.)
'at every turn of its furious course Charlotte Brontë's imagination throws off some such glinting spark of phrase. And now and again the sparks blaze up into a sustained passage of De Quinceyish prose poetry.' (Ibid., p. 111.)
'their strange flame [i.e. writers like Charlotte Brontë], lit as it is at the central white hot fire of creative inspiration, will in every age find them followers.' (Ibid., p. 114.)

Virginia Woolf, another impressionistic critic, also invokes 'fire' in her short essay on *Jane Eyre*:

'I could never rest in communication with strong, discreet and refined minds', she [Charlotte] writes, as any leader-writer in a provincial journal might have written; but gathering fire and speed goes on in her own authentic voice, 'till I had passed the outworks of conventional reserve and won a place by their hearts' very hearthstone.' It is there that she takes her seat; it is the red and fitful glow of the heart's fire which illumines her page. (*The Common Reader*, Penguin edn (1938), p. 157.)

3. Here a computer would be useful. But I have been obliged to use clumsier and more laborious methods, for which I do not claim 100% accuracy. Any errors, however, will not in general have assisted my arguments: I may have missed some occurrences of a particular linguistic element in a particular text, but I have not invented any.

4. See Raymond Williams, *Reading and Criticism* (1950), pp. 75–86, for a useful analysis of *Heart of Darkness* along these lines.

5. David Daiches, *Virginia Woolf* (1945), pp. 64–5 and 72. The illustration, like the two following, is from *Mrs Dalloway*.

6. Daiches, p. 71.

7. Ibid., p. 72.

8. I have stated it all provisionally because it is not to my present purpose to sustain it in detail.

Norman Page 'Forms of Speech in Fiction' (1973)

. . . At every point at which a novelist wishes to convey an impression of the use of speech, he is forced to make a conscious or unconscious choice between the various forms available. (Not every form, of course, has been equally at the disposal of every generation.) If we assume for the moment a hypothetical notion of the 'actual words spoken' in the fictional world of his creation, his choice will determine how close to, or how remote from, those 'actual words spoken' his presentation of speech will be. He may decide to adopt the role of the dramatist and, by the use of direct speech, to allow his characters to 'speak for themselves'.

DIRECT SPEECH

There is usually no problem in recognising direct speech, consisting as it does of the actual words the reader is to suppose to have been uttered by a character in dialogue, monologue or soliloquy, and normally accompanied by the appropriate graphological indications (though these, as examples from the *Authorized Version* to Joyce's *Ulysses* show, are by no means indispensable). The various indications of direct speech have been described as 'invitations to an auditory experience',[1] but this description needs modification to suggest that what is in question is, rather, the provision of hints towards an imaginative reconstruction of speech by the reader on the basis of his empirical knowledge of speech and his familiarity with the conventions of written dialogue. The psycholinguistic question of what *happens* when various readers (silently) read a passage of dialogue – of how the experience differs, on the one hand, from hearing speech and, on the other, from reading passages of non-dialogue prose – is a fascinating and complex one. Probably there is considerable variation between individuals, related to (among other things) reading speed and accuracy of aural memory, as well as an important degree of difference according to the writer's mode of presentation.

In its purest form a passage may consist so largely of direct speech, so little diluted with other elements, as to resemble an extract from a play. (The quotations from Hemingway and Compton-Burnett in the last chapter belong to this category.)

This is perhaps the point to recall, even at the expense of a brief digression, that the English novel drew a considerable portion of its sustenance in the earlier phases of its development from the drama. Defoe, in *Roxana*, *Colonel Jack*, and other novels, habitually set out his dialogue in dramatic form; Richardson was very fond of what he described as 'the rational diversion of a good play' and, according to a recent critic, 'got a diversity of techniques and materials from his knowledge of plays';[2] Fielding, like Dickens and Henry James later, wrote for the stage as well as the novel-reader, and his experience as a comic dramatist can be traced in the deft handling of situation and dialogue in many scenes of *Tom Jones*. The tradition is a continuous one: in our own time, Graham Greene, Angus Wilson, William Golding and Muriel Spark among others have written for stage, film or radio. Moreover, the novel in the course of its history usurped some of the social functions of the theatre, the rise of the former being accompanied by the decline of the latter. The greatest period of the English novel, the Victorian age, is also that in which the native drama sank almost into insignificance. In the eighteenth-century novel, when the art of fiction is still in the process of discovering its own techniques and is therefore apt to lean most heavily on established genres, the reader often has the sense of the novelist providing equivalents for theatrical elements which must necessarily, in the novel medium, be rendered verbally. Thus passages of description replace the direct visual impact of scenery, costumes, and the movements of the actors, and narrative is a natural development from stage-directions.[3]

It is in dialogue, of course, that the two genres approximate most closely to each other, and where the art of the dramatist could be transferred with a minimum of adaptation to the novel. Many scenes in Richardson and Fielding suggest that they were conceived in terms of the stage. However, the advantages of the novel-medium in being able to present, in constantly varying proportions, both dialogue and as much or as little complementary and supplementary description, information or comment as the author may desire, are too real to be disregarded. *Direct Speech* is generally accompanied, therefore, by some or all of the following:

[1] attributions to speakers, often necessary to avoid confusion or tedious calculation on the reader's part, and an obvious example of a substitution for an element provided in the theatre by the physical presence of the actors. It may be noted that many writers seek to relieve the monotony of constant 'he-saids' by resorting to elegant variation, though the variations, when not simply a novelistic habit, are in themselves expressive. The opening chapter of *David Copperfield* has *returned* eight times, *asked* and *cried* five times each, *exclaimed*, *faltered* and *resumed* twice each, and *repeated*, *replied*, *sobbed*, *mused* and *ejaculating* once each, as well as *said* thirty-seven times; only two very short sentences are not explicitly attributed to a speaker.

[2] 'stage-directions' as to facial expression, movement, gesture, etc – the expressive accompaniments of speech. The theatrical element in the eighteenth-century novel has already been referred to, and in Fielding such 'stage-directions' are often introduced into a passage of speech as they might be into a dramatic script: thus Lady Booby in *Joseph Andrews* recalls her dead husband, saying that

'. . . the dear man who is gone' (*here she began to sob*), 'was he alive again' (*then she produced tears*), 'could not upbraid me with any one act of tenderness or passion.'

Naturally enough, the practice of different novelists in this respect varies widely, in accordance with the extent to which their dialogue is conceived in dramatic and visual terms. Jane Austen, for example, who is more concerned with the moral implications of a scene than with rendering its circumstantiality, uses them sparingly, whereas they are abundant in Dickens, as the often-noted theatrical element in his work would lead one to expect. Related to them are

[3] references to or indications of paralinguistic qualities such as stress, pitch, intonation, volume, vocal quality, either within the dialogue itself (by, for instance, such devices as capitalisation, italicisation and hyphenation) or in the accompanying comments ('he muttered', 'she shrieked', etc). To draw attention to them by direct comment is to throw the major burden of reconstructing a particular variety of speech upon the reader, for an indication such as 'he lisped' will serve little purpose in the dialogue unless the reader is prepared to take it into account in his inner experience of reading it, just as he is required to reproduce the appropriate behaviour from his own observation and memory if he is reading the passage aloud. By well-established convention, a single indication of this kind permits the dialogue itself to be given 'straight', that is, without further formal indications of eccentricity. The method has the obvious advantage of being less troublesome for both author and reader: the lispings of Mr Sleary in *Hard Times* not only gave Dickens a good deal of trouble (as his manuscript makes plain) but can quickly prove irksome and tedious in the reading, since they are permitted to interfere with normal orthography to the extent of slowing down the reader considerably. On the other hand, they do virtually compel the reader to 'listen' to Mr Sleary, even if he is reading silently. Another advantage of the once-and-for-all indication outside the dialogue itself is that it can enable the writer to suggest features of speech which the written language is not equipped to represent adequately – an inflection or tone that may be meaningful but quite beyond the power of the printer's symbols to convey. How, for example, could such favourite formulae attached to dialogue as 'he chuckled' or 'she hinted darkly' be otherwise rendered? The major disadvantage of the method lies in the surrender of the comic or dramatic possibilities of eccentric dialogue, and in the risk that the rapid or careless reader may completely overlook the characteristic in question. Emily Brontë's persistence in rendering the Yorkshire dialect of Joseph, already illustrated, makes a contribution to the grotesque and uncouth impression created

by this character in *Wuthering Heights* that could scarcely have been achieved by a simple reference to his broad local dialect. (At the same time, one might well enquire what would be the effect of Joseph's speech on, say, an Australian or West African reader totally unfamiliar with West Riding speech, and whether the internal representation of his pronunciation achieves something that could not otherwise have been obtained.) The two different methods may be illustrated by contrasting two passages by Dickens. When Mr Pecksniff is intoxicated (*Martin Chuzzlewit*, ch. 9), we are told that he speaks 'with imperfect articulation', and there are subsequent reminders of his condition in references to his 'thick and husky voice' and his 'stuttering', but the dialogue itself bears no orthographic or other evidence of this state. David Copperfield's inebriation, on the other hand, is manifested both within and outside the dialogue: '"Agnes?" I said thickly, "Lorblessmer! Agnes!"' (*David Copperfield*, ch. 24). There can be little doubt which example arrests the reader's attention more readily by its linguistic vitality.

[4] finally, many novelists find the temptation to interpolate comment or moralising into dialogue passages quite irresistible. Perhaps none goes further in this respect than Sterne in *Tristram Shandy*: in the famous scene in which Bobby's death is reported to the servants by Corporal Trim (Bk V, ch. 7), the dialogue is almost submerged by the tide of commentary and analysis.

The use of direct speech within a given episode may be conveniently illustrated from the trial scene in the thirty-fourth chapter of *The Pickwick Papers* (with special attention to the passage from 'The judge had no sooner taken his seat . . .' to '. . . out of court'). Its dramatic quality, in its use of speech to reveal character as well as further the action, is evident, and it later became one of Dickens's most successful public readings. Well over half the passage in question consists of direct speech, and there is a generous use of what have been loosely referred to as 'stage directions': 'with interesting agitation', 'with a cunning look', etc. At the same time one notes several useful devices which are not at the dramatist's disposal. A phrase such as 'after a few unimportant questions' enables the novelist to dispense with a potentially low-pressure stretch of dialogue in a way that would be difficult to achieve on the stage. Similarly, we are told that 'Mrs Cluppins repeated the conversation with which our readers are already acquainted', and 'our readers' are accordingly not subjected to the tedium of repetition. Again, the browbeating of Mr Winkle is presented with notable economy by the partial use of indirect speech, which also provides stylistic variety. Although the scene contains, therefore, a high proportion of direct speech – and it is significant that when Dickens came to prepare his reading version very few changes were necessary to turn the novel-text into a dramatic script – the novelist has taken advantage of the possibilities of manipulating the tempo of his episode and the angle of its presentation in a manner that belongs distinctively to the written medium.

Three common conventions in the use of direct speech should be briefly referred to. One is the custom of reproducing dialogue, even in a first-person narrative, without any reservations as to its accuracy or completeness: thus, conversations which are supposed to have taken place many years earlier are often given intact in all their details. This species of total recall on the narrator's part is a natural, and easily-accepted, convention of the medium. A more technical convention relates to the expectations aroused by the use of quotation marks and other graphological and typographical indications that 'actual speech' is being offered. In earlier periods, and certainly until the beginning of the nineteenth century, quotation marks were used in certain contexts where they would not nowadays be employed. In Fielding, for example, we find the following:

Meeting the landlady, he accosted her with great civility, and asked 'What he could have for dinner?'   [*Tom Jones*, VIII, 4]

The usage is found as late as Jane Austen, but by the time of Dickens the quotation marks have disappeared:

He checks his horse and asks a workman does he know the name of Rouncewell thereabouts?   [*Bleak House*, ch. 63]

Such examples, though not identical in grammatical structure, show a common movement towards the integration of direct speech with narrative style – a tendency to which we must shortly turn. There remains to be noted a third convention, much favoured by Jane Austen, whereby the novelist is permitted to conflate into a single speech what must probably be supposed to have been uttered as several separate speeches. The gain in speed and concentration of effect is considerable. Consider, for example, Mr Woodhouse's characteristic expressions of anxiety in the third chapter of *Emma*:

> 'Mrs Bates, let me propose your venturing on one of these eggs. An egg boiled very soft is not unwholesome. Serle understands boiling an egg better than anybody . . . Miss Bates, let Emma help you to a *little* bit of tart – a *very* little bit. Ours are all apple-tarts. You need not be afraid of unwholesome preserves here. I do not advise the custard. Mrs Goddard, what say you to *half* a glass of wine? A *small* half glass, put into a tumbler of water? . . .'

Jane Austen has caught the timidity of Mr Woodhouse in the face of experience, even experience taking the mild form of an apple-tart, and has found linguistic equivalents for it in his speech, with its repeated negatives and diminutives. It seems unlikely, however, that this would have been delivered as an uninterrupted monologue, since Woodhouse addresses three ladies in turn, of whom Miss Bates at least would hardly have remained silent; and the passage quoted might well have been presented as three separate speeches with appropriate responses interspersed. More important than these unreported replies, however, is the cumulative effect of the old gentleman's frettings, and his conversation is presented as monologue in the interests of clarity of character-portrayal. A more glaring example, which invites comparison with the final speech of Marlowe's *Dr Faustus*, occurs in *Northanger Abbey*. Anxiously awaiting her friends, and hearing the clock strike twelve, Catherine Morland declares:

> 'I do not quite despair yet. I shall not give it up till a quarter after twelve. This is just the time of day for it to clear up, and I do think it looks a little lighter. There, it is twenty minutes after twelve, and now I *shall* give it up entirely . . .'

Unblushingly, the novelist permits twenty minutes to elapse

during the uttering of less than forty words. Quite clearly, the force of the quotation marks in this example is different from that in most direct speech: a protracted conversation, or at least a one-sided series of remarks, has been telescoped into a single speech in the interests of narrative economy. By such means can the tendency to diffuseness inherent in the use of direct speech be circumvented. A different kind of convention operates in the vulgar Mrs Elton's raptures over the strawberry-picking (*Emma*, ch. 42):

'The best fruit in England – every body's favourite – always wholesome. These the finest beds and finest sorts. – Delightful to gather for one's self – the only way of really enjoying them . . .'

– and so on, at considerable length. The gist of many long and tedious speeches is conveyed through a drastically abridged monologue, involving the sacrifice of most of the main verbs – the abridgement itself implying an ironic comment on the speaker's wearisome volubility. As with Miss Bates in the same novel, we have the impression of tedium without suffering its effects. Again, although we cannot suppose that Mrs Elton would continue at such length without even the encouragement of a sympathetic murmur, all other participants in the conversation have been eliminated, so that what we encounter is not so much a transcript of a supposed dialogue as a heavily edited version of it. With this last example, indeed, we begin to move away from direct speech proper in the direction of the freer forms.

Direct speech, therefore, is not a single method but can range from the undoctored to the stylised, though its distinctive virtue lies in its capacity for allowing a character to 'speak', in an individual voice, directly to the reader without the appearance of authorial intervention. Its advantages are its immediacy and the stylistic variety attainable in dialogue which can offer lexical and syntactical contrasts to the other portions of a novel; its limitations are a tendency towards diffuseness and a consequent thinness of effect, and the need for frequent 'gear-shifting' – not always easily accomplished – in the change from non-dialogue to dialogue elements and back again.

INDIRECT SPEECH

Indirect speech can offer a gain in pace and economy by way of compensation for the loss of immediacy; it also combines more readily with narrative style, making possible a free movement from one to the other. But even less than the direct variety is indirect speech a single, unvarying form. Although it traditionally employs (in parliamentary reporting, for example) a neutral style, it need not in the novel necessarily involve a total renunciation of the attempt to represent individual varieties of speech. It can assume some of the normal features of the indirect form whilst retaining others which belong to the direct form. Thus we need to be aware of 'degrees of indirectness', some sense of which may be appreciated by considering the differences displayed by a handful of brief quotations:

1 Lydia was bid by her two eldest sisters to hold her tongue . . . Turning to Mr Bennet, he (Mr Collins) offered himself as his antagonist at backgammon.   [Austen, *Pride and Prejudice*, ch. 14]

2 Mrs Bickerton assured her, that the acceptance of any reckoning was entirely out of the question . . .   [Scott, *The Heart of Midlothian*, ch. 28]

3 The doctor accused Mr Allworthy of too great lenity, repeated his accusations against his brother, and declared that he should never more be brought either to see, or to own him for his relation.

[Fielding, *Tom Jones*, I, ch. 12]

4 Mr Sapsea expressed his opinion that the case had a dark look; in short (and here his eyes rested full on Neville's countenance), an un-English complexion.   [Dickens, *Edwin Drood*, ch. 15]

5 Mrs O'Dowd [described] how it had been presented to her by her fawther, as she stipt into the car'ge after her mar'ge.

[Thackeray, *Vanity Fair*, ch. 28]

Of all these extracts, each of which implies the use of speech by a named character, we may ask the same question: To what extent may the 'original words spoken' be reconstructed from the indirect form? The answers given will be very different, however. The examples from Austen belong to narrative style, though there is a clear indication that speech has taken place. The reader has no means of reconstructing the specific stylistic features of the 'original' utterances; and though it is quite conceivable that the pompous Mr Collins should have proposed a game by offering himself as an 'antagonist', and equally likely that one or both of Lydia's sisters used the unladylike expression 'hold your tongue', these expressions may equally possibly belong only to the narrative style and in no way imply a verbal echo of the speeches that lie behind it. The reader is simply not in a position to know. What saves the question from being purely pedantic is the not unimportant matter of how far a given style enables the reader to 'hear' a distinctive speaking voice which, by its particular qualities, contributes to dramatic situation and character-development. What we have here is not indirect speech in the ordinary sense, but what might be termed 'submerged speech': the supposed dialogue has become absorbed by the narrative, with consequent likely changes of lexis as well as a grammatical form different from that of indirect speech (since it lacks the subordinate clause or clauses dependent on a verb of saying). It thus differs from the example in (2), which belongs to the category of ordinary or traditional indirect speech: the main clause identifies the speaker and includes the verb of saying, whilst the subordinate clause conveys the substance of the speech and involves a tense-shift (in this case, from present to past). But this indirect version bears little stylistic evidence of the colloquial origin of the speech reported, since the landlady's remark has become subdued to the formal style of Scott's narrative. This we may regard as indirect speech proper, in which a neutral reporting style irons out the possible eccentricities of the individual 'original' speeches.

The next example combines the two forms already identified. The first half of Fielding's sentence (to 'brother') indicates summarily the content of what was obviously a speech of some length, but the second half moves from editorial summary to indirect speech as defined above. A new element is found in the sentence from *Edwin Drood*, which seems to bear the outward tokens of indirect speech but is significantly different from the earlier example from Scott. In its subordinate clause it forsakes a neutral reporting style and, for the sake of the wordplay, reproduces the phrases 'a dark look' and 'an un-English complexion' intact from the direct speech implied. In this case, therefore, the use of indirect speech does not prevent the reader from 'hearing' Mr Sapsea in his individuality and does not entail an inevitable sacrifice of immediacy and vividness. Finally, the quotation from Thackeray shows that features of phonology as well as of lexis and syntax are within its scope: even the orthography of the indirect version is susceptible to 'colouring' by the Anglo-Irish pronunciation of Mrs O'Dowd.

In the light of examples such as these, the simple and attractive antithesis that 'Direct speech is natural speech. Indirect speech is artificial speech'[4] is hardly acceptable in relation to the novel. Such an antithesis only obscures the considerable common element which exists *between* the two kinds, as well as the varieties distinguishable *within* each kind. In the whole question of forms of speech-presentation, indeed, what is encountered is not so much a set of rigid categories, each with its own exclusive and unmistakable identifying features, as a merging of one form with another and with narrative style. Nor, though the question has traditionally been treated as a grammatical one, can the placing of a particular instance always be made solely on the basis of grammatical features. As suggested above, the need exists to distinguish further between at least two kinds of indirect speech: that which enables the reader to deduce some of the structural and lexical features of the original, and that in which these features have become absorbed by the style deemed appropriate for the reported version. For the purposes of illustration, and to show that there are further 'degrees of indirectness' which need to be distinguished within each of these two kinds, the simple exercise may be performed of recasting a single short speech in several different ways. In chapter 25 of Dickens's *Martin Chuzzlewit* we find the following example of direct speech:

'There are some happy creeturs', Mrs Gamp observed, 'as time runs back'ards with, and you are one, Mrs Mould . . .'

This possesses certain features which may be regarded as contributing to the peculiar vitality and variety of direct speech: non-standard grammar to suggest a particular social dialect, variant spellings to suggest distinctive qualities of pronunciation, the use of a form of address. We may ask to what extent these may be preserved in the various forms of indirect speech. To begin at the point remotest from the original: the sentence might have been presented as what has been termed 'submerged speech', in some such form as

1 Mrs Gamp complimented Mrs Mould on her youthful appearance.

This indicates that speech has taken place but retains none of the idiosyncrasies of the original: lexically, it is formal and literary; grammatically, it is beyond reproach; and there is no implication of non-standard pronunciation. Or it might have appeared as indirect speech in any one of a number of ways. For example:

2 Mrs Gamp observed that some fortunate people, of whom Mrs Mould was one, seemed to be unaffected by time.
3 Mrs Gamp observed that there were some happy creatures that time ran backwards with, and that Mrs Mould was one of them.
4 Mrs Gamp observed that there were some happy creeturs as time ran back'ards with, and that Mrs Mould was one of them.

All of these follow the normal structural conventions of indirect speech (verb of saying + that (may be omitted) + subordinate clause with verb in past tense and pronouns in third person); but they stand at varying distances from the direct speech on which they are based. (2) is farthest from it, and amounts to a virtual paraphrase: syntax apart, it has much in common with (1). (4), on the other hand, preserves many features of the original, including its orthographic variants, and may be conveniently referred to as 'coloured' or 'modified' indirect speech. (3) falls between these two extremes, and may perhaps reasonably be termed 'parallel indirect speech', on account of its lexical faithfulness to the original. There are, of course, many other possible variations, but only two call for special mention:

5 There were some happy creatures that time ran backwards with, and Mrs Mould was one of them.
6 Mrs Gamp observed that there were some happy creatures that time ran backwards with, 'and you are one, Mrs Mould'.

In (5) the use of *free* indirect speech is characterised by the absence of indication of speaker. (A further variation would be to modify this version by reproducing the original spelling of *creeturs* and *back'ards*.) In (6) we have an example of what has been termed 'slipping' from indirect into direct speech[5] – the character's voice interrupting the narrator's, as it were; again a further variation is possible by the omission of the quotation marks.

The main features of the various forms so far identified may be summarised as shown in the table (below).

Type of speech	Grammatical features		Lexical features	
	1 introductory verb of saying (usually that)	2 subordinate clause in past tense	1 neutral or idiosyncratic[a]	2 possible indicatio of phonological qualities
A: Direct	no	no	idiosyncratic	yes
B: 'Submerged'	yes	no	neutral	no
C: Indirect	yes	yes	neutral	no[b]
D: 'Parallel' indirect	yes	yes	idiosyncratic	no
E: 'Coloured' indirect	yes	yes	idiosyncratic	yes
F: Free indirect	no	no	idiosyncratic	no
G: Free direct[c]	no	no	idiosyncratic	yes

H: 'Slipping' from indirect into direct speech involves a mid-sentence change from C to A.

a 'Neutral': lexically undifferentiated with regard to the individual speaker. 'Idiosyncratic': reflecting the qualities (often grammatical as well as lexical) of the 'original' speech.
b Or, exceptionally, 'yes', as in the example from *Vanity Fair*.
c Graphological indications of direct speech are also omitted; this form seems relatively rare in English (see L. C. Harmer, *The French Language Today*, 1954, pp. 300–1).

Free indirect speech, briefly referred to above, now calls for further discussion. Though identified and discussed by linguists only in this century, free indirect speech (also known as *style indirect libre* and *erlebte Rede*) is used by a number of nineteenth-century authors from Jane Austen onwards.[6] An even earlier example occurs in a novel Jane Austen knew well, Fanny Burney's *Evelina* (1778):

. . . Lord Orville saw and approached me.
    He begged to know if I was not well?
    He then . . . asked if he had been so unhappy as to offend me?
    'No, indeed!' cried I; and . . . I desired to know if he had seen the young
lady who had been conversing with me?
    No; – but would I honour him with my commands to see her?
    'O, by no means!'
    Was there any other person with whom I wished to speak? . . .

                                                    [*Evelina*, Letter XI; my italics]

In this short passage we find an interesting combination of
direct speech (reserved for the heroine-narrator), indirect
speech, and free indirect speech (italicised) for Lord Orville's
later remarks. The author's purpose seems to be to retain her
heroine as the centre of attention by permitting Evelina's
narrating 'voice' to continue without interruption: Orville is
distanced since both the indirect and the free indirect forms
serve a common aim of mediating his remarks through
Evelina, but the switch from indirect to free indirect marks a
slight but perceptible rise in dramatic urgency.

Jane Austen's usage goes well beyond anything to be found
in Fanny Burney, and may be briefly illustrated from
Persuasion (1818) – a novel in which she can be seen to have
moved towards a remarkably flexible conception of speech-
presentation.[7] Both examples occur in the same passage in
chapter 20:

. . . she found herself accosted by Captain Wentworth, in a reserved yet
hurried sort of farewell. 'He must wish her good night. He was going – he
should get home as fast as he could.'

. . . But alas! there were very different thoughts to succeed. How was such
jealousy to be quieted? How was the truth to reach him? How, in all the
peculiar disadvantages of their respective situations, would he ever learn her
real sentiments?

The first of these follows eighteenth-century practice in
enclosing the substance of Wentworth's speech in quotation
marks, though it is clearly not his 'actual words' that we are
given. The use of free indirect speech here, in place of the more
usual direct form, has the effect of merging dialogue with
narrative and retaining the consistent viewpoint of the heroine,
whose emotional state remains the centre of attention. Part of

the smoothness of the transition from narrative to speech is owed to the fact that the first- and second-person pronouns of direct speech can, in free indirect speech, appear as the third-person pronouns normal in narrative. At the same time, the brief, urgent statements have the dramatic impact of direct speech, the syntax suggesting dialogue rather than formal narrative prose. In the second example, thoughts rather than speech are in question: Anne Elliot's reflections are given through free indirect speech without quotation marks, but the implication is clearly on the lines of 'Anne wondered how . . .' The reader is given an insight into her consciousness that is the fictional equivalent of the dramatic soliloquy, yet the narrative voice remains in command (compare the artificiality of the effect obtained by another soliloquising heroine, Hardy's Eustacia Vye in *The Return of the Native*, Bk V, ch. 7 of which offers a good example). Present-tense verbs move into the past, and *our* and *my* become *their* and *her*. This last instance well illustrates Ullmann's comment that free indirect speech 'supersedes the borderline between narrative and inner speech, so that the two imperceptibly merge into one another'.

It is now clear that free indirect speech offers the novelist the opportunity to combine some of the separate advantages of both the direct and the indirect forms. Pointing out that it 'has some features in common with both of the orthodox types', Ullmann enumerates the following as among its more usual characteristics.[8] (Although he is, in the discussion referred to, concerned with French style, most of his account applies with equal force to English usages.)

[1] Transposition of verbs: as in indirect speech, if the narrative is in the past tense, the verbs will change, the present becoming the preterite, the preterite the pluperfect, etc, though it is possible to find exceptions to this.

[2] Transposition of pronouns: again as in indirect speech, first and second persons change to third.

[3] Absence of subordination: each sentence appears as an independent unit, not a subordinate clause, so that there is no 'key-verb' on which it is syntactically dependent.

[4] Preservation of such 'emotive elements' as questions,

exclamations, interjections, colloquial language, slang and vulgar terms, together with an attempt to imitate 'the inflexions and intonations of the speaking voice'.

Of these, the most important in terms of literary effect is the last, offering as it does almost unlimited possibilities of stylistic variety without the necessity of transition to the sometimes cumbrous and uneconomical mode of direct speech.

Later nineteenth-century novelists were not slow to discover the usefulness of the free indirect form. Another quotation from *Edwin Drood* (1870) will reveal the smoothness and pace it can permit:

. . . she feels it much more to the purpose to encourage him. And she does encourage him.	*narrative*
He will write to her? He will write to her every alternate day, and tell her all his adventures. Does he send clothes on in advance of him?	*free indirect speech*
'My dear Helena, no. Travel like a pilgrim, with wallet and staff . . . and here is my staff!'	*direct speech*
He hands it to her; she makes the same remark as Mr Crisparkle, that it is very heavy; and gives it back to him, asking what wood it is? Ironwood.	*narrative; indirect speech; free indirect speech (or free direct speech?)*

This dialogue between Neville Landless and his sister includes within a few lines both direct and indirect as well as free indirect (and perhaps free direct) speech. (The free indirect speech shows in this case the changes of person, but not the changes of tense, already noted as customary.) It achieves an admirable briskness by the omission of explicit indications of speaker and by free movement between different modes of speech-presentation. Furthermore, it contrives to present dialogue without abdication of the narrator's role as story-teller: although the 'voices' of Neville and Helena are given a hearing, it is the authorial 'voice' which remains dominant throughout. . . .

SOURCE: extract from *Speech in the English Novel* (London, 1973), pp. 24–38.

NOTES

1. M. Gregory, 'Aspects of Varieties Differentiation', *Journal of Linguistics*, III (1967), p. 193.

2. G. Sherburn, 'Samuel Richardson's Novels and the Theatre: A Theory Sketched', *Philological Quarterly*, XLI (1962), p. 325.

3. Cf. W. Raleigh, *The English Novel* (London, 1894), p. 142.

4. B. Blackstone, *Indirect Speech: Its Principles and Practice* (London, 1962), p. 1.

5. Cf. G. L. Schuelke, ' "Slipping" in Indirect Discourse', *American Speech*, XXXIII (1958), pp. 90–8.

6. Cf. L. Glauser, *Die erlebte Rede im englischen Roman des 19. Jahrhunderts* (Zürich, 1948), which examines the use of free indirect speech by eight nineteenth-century English novelists. See also M. Lips, *Le style indirect libre* (Paris, 1926) and S. Ullmann, *Style in the French Novel* (Cambridge, 1957), ch. 2.

7. Cf. N. Page, 'Categories of Speech in *Persuasion*', *Modern Language Review*, LXIV (1969), pp. 734–41.

8. S. Ullmann, op. cit. pp. 97–9.

PART THREE
Authors and Texts

Caroline Spurgeon 'The Imagery of *Hamlet*' (1935)

. . . In *Hamlet*, naturally, we find ourselves in an entirely different atmosphere [from that of *Romeo and Juliet*]. If we look closely we see this is partly due to the number of images of sickness, disease or blemish of the body, in the play. . . , and we discover that the idea of an ulcer or tumour, as descriptive of the unwholesome condition of Denmark morally, is, on the whole, the dominating one.

Hamlet speaks of his mother's sin as a blister on the 'fair forehead of an innocent love', she speaks of her 'sick soul', and as in *King Lear* the emotion is so strong and the picture so vivid, that the metaphor overflows into the verbs and adjectives: heaven's face, he tells her, is *thought-sick* at the act; her husband is a *mildew'd ear, blasting his wholesome* brother; to have married him, her sense must be not only *sickly*, but *apoplex'd*. Finally, at the end of that terrific scene (III 4], he implores her not to soothe herself with the belief that his father's apparition is due to her son's madness, and not to her own guilt, for that

> will but skin and film the ulcerous place,
> Whiles rank corruption, mining all within,
> Infects unseen.

So also, later, he compares the unnecessary fighting between Norway and Poland to a kind of tumour which grows out of too much prosperity. He sees the country and the people in it alike in terms of a sick body needing medicine or the surgeon's knife. When he surprises Claudius at his prayers, he exclaims,

> This physic but prolongs thy sickly days;

and he describes the action of conscience in the unforgettable picture of the healthy, ruddy countenance turning pale with sickness. A mote in the eye, a 'vicious mole', a galled chilblain, a probed wound and purgation, are also among Hamlet's images; and the mind of Claudius runs equally on the same theme.

When he hears of the murder of Polonius, he declares that his weakness in not sooner having had Hamlet shut up was comparable to the cowardly action of a man with a 'foul disease' who

> To keep it from divulging, let it feed
> Even on the pith of life;

and later, when arranging to send Hamlet to England and to his death, he justifies it by the proverbial tag:

> diseases desperate grown
> By desperate appliance are relieved,
> Or not at all;

and adjures the English king to carry out his behest, in the words of a fever patient seeking a sedative:

> For like the hectic in my blood he rages,
> And thou must cure me.

When working on Laertes, so that he will easily fall in with the design for the fencing match, his speech is full of the same underlying thought of a body sick, or ill at ease:

> goodness, growing to a plurisy,
> Dies in his own too much;

and finally, he sums up the essence of the position and its urgency with lightning vividness in a short medical phrase:

> But, to the quick o' the ulcer:
> Hamlet comes back.

In marked contrast to *King Lear*, though bodily disease is emphasised, bodily action and strain are little drawn upon; indeed, only in Hamlet's great speech are they brought before us at all (*to be shot at* with slings and arrows, *to take arms against* troubles and *oppose* them, *to suffer* shocks, *to bear* the lash of whips, and *endure* pangs, *to grunt* and *sweat* under burdens, and so on), and here, as in *King Lear*, they serve to intensify the feeling of mental anguish. In *Hamlet*, however, anguish is not the dominating thought, but *rottenness*, disease, corruption, the result of *dirt*; the people are 'muddied' – 'Thick and unwholesome in their thoughts and whispers' – and this corruption is, in the words of Claudius, 'rank' and 'smells to heaven', so that the state of things in Denmark which shocks, paralyses and finally overwhelms Hamlet, is as the foul tumour breaking inwardly and poisoning the whole body, while showing 'no cause without/Why the man dies.'

This image pictures and reflects not only the outward condition which causes Hamlet's spiritual illness, but also his own state. Indeed, the shock of the discovery of his father's murder and the sight of his mother's conduct have been such that when the play opens Hamlet has already begun to die, to die internally; because all the springs of life – love, laughter, joy, hope, belief in others – are becoming frozen at their source, are being gradually infected by the disease of the spirit which is – unknown to him – killing him.

To Shakespeare's pictorial imagination, therefore, the problem in *Hamlet* is not predominantly that of will and reason, of a mind too philosophic or a nature temperamentally unfitted to act quickly; he sees it pictorially *not as the problem of an individual at all*, but as something greater and even more mysterious, as a *condition* for which the individual himself is apparently not responsible, any more than the sick man is to blame for the infection which strikes and devours him, but which, nevertheless, in its course and development, impartially and relentlessly, annihilates him and others, innocent and guilty alike. That is the tragedy of *Hamlet*, as it is perhaps the chief tragic mystery of life. . . .

SOURCE: extract from *Shakespeare's Imagery and What It Tells Us* (Cambridge, 1935), pp. 316–19.

M. M. Mahood   'Shakespeare's Wordplay' (1957)

Wordplay was a game the Elizabethans played seriously. Shakespeare's first audience would have found a noble climax in the conclusion of Mark Antony's lament over Caesar:

> O World! thou wast the Forrest to this *Hart*,
> And this indeed, O World, the *Hart* of thee,

just as they would have relished the earnest pun of Hamlet's reproach to Gertrude:

> Could you on this faire Mountaine leaue to feed,
> And batten on this *Moore*?

To Elizabethan ways of thinking, there was plenty of authority for those eloquent devices. It was to be found in Scripture (*Tu es Petrus . . .*) and in the whole line of rhetoricians, from Aristotle and Quintilian, through the neo-classical textbooks that Shakespeare read perforce at school, to the English writers such as Puttenham whom he read later for his own advantage as a poet. Dr Johnson's protest that a quibble was to Shakespeare 'the fatal Cleopatra for which he lost the world and was content to lose it' itself contains a pregnant quibble. Cleopatra was fatal in being both the death and destiny of Antony; and however Shakespeare's puns may have endangered his reputation with the Augustans, he was destined by his age and education to play with words.

Puns were repugnant to Johnson because a linguistic revolution as far-reaching in its effects as the Great Rebellion separated his verbal habits from Shakespeare's. Half a century after Shakespeare's death, Eachard put forward as a possible reform in education: 'Whether or no Punning, Quibling, and that which they call Joquing, and such other delicaces of Wit, highly admired in some Academick Exercises, might not be very conveniently omitted?'[1] The great aim of Eachard and his contemporaries was to make language perspicuous. It had accordingly to be free of such prismatic devices as synonyms, metaphors and puns, Eachard sought to drive puns from the pulpit, Cowley's *Ode on Wit* celebrated their explusion from poetry and the *Spectator* tried to blackmail their admission to Augustan society – to judge from the conversation of Swift and his friends, with small success.

Johnson's 'great contempt for that species of wit' is the aftermath of this Augustan cult of correctness and *le mot juste*. Yet Johnson's experience as a lexicographer quickened his response to the alternative meanings of words. The alertness which makes him spot (to give one example) the wordplay on *planta pedis* in 'some o' their *Plants* are ill rooted already' [*Antony and Cleopatra*, II vii 1–2] will not allow more serious punning to pass unnoticed. 'Perhaps here is a poor jest intended between *mood* the *mind* and *moods* of musick' in Cleopatra's

> Giue me some Musicke: Musicke, moody foode of
> vs that trade in Loue,   [II v 1–2]

and while he is 'loath to think that *Shakespeare* meant to play with the double of *match* for *nuptial*, and the *match* of a *gun*' he does nevertheless respond to the Citizen's pun in *King John*:

> for at this *match*,
> With swifter spleene then power can enforce
> The mouth of passage shall we fling wide ope,
> And giue you entrance.   [II i 447–50]

Although Johnson occasionally finds a quibble which is not allowed by modern editors – as in *Richard III*: 'You meane to beare me, not to beare with me' [III i 128], where he sees an improbable pun on *bear* the animal – he deserves our thanks for his quick response to Shakespeare's wordplay instead of the blame he sometimes gets for failing to appreciate it. He shows far more perception in the matter than the nineteenth-century commentators. Shakespeare's Victorian editors, whose conflicting interpretations swell the *Variorum* edition, seldom saw[2] that all meanings of a word might be admissible even though some must take precedence over others. The pun's credit was very low in the last century, in spite of Coleridge's repeated efforts to justify Shakespeare's puns on psychological grounds. Byron's attempts to revive a Shakespearean form of wordplay were little to the taste of the Victorians; and their own wordplay, if it surpassed the cracker-motto ingenuity of Hood, whose Fatal Cleopatra

> died, historians relate,
> Through having found a misplaced asp-irate,

had to hide in the nursery. Jabberwocky could be enjoyed only at seven and a half exactly.

Since then, Addison's worst fears have been realised; we have 'degenerated into a race of punsters'. Where the Augustans disapproved of Shakespeare's wordplay and the Victorians ignored it, we now acclaim it. A generation that relishes *Finnegans Wake* is more in danger of reading non-existent quibbles into Shakespeare's work than of missing his subtlest play of meaning. Shakespearean criticism today recognises wordplay as a major poetic device, comparable in its effectiveness with the use of recurrent or clustered images. . . .

SOURCE: extract from *Shakespeare's Wordplay* (London, 1957), pp. 9–11.

NOTES

[Renumbered from the original – Ed.]

1. Eachard, *The Ground and Occasions of the Contempt of the Clergy* (1670), p. 33.

2. Except unconsciously. See William Empson, *Seven Types of Ambiguity* (1947), pp. 81–2.

Angus McIntosh   *As You Like It*: A Grammatical Clue to Character (1963)

The main qualities of the overtones carried by the pronouns *thou* and *you* in Shakespeare's time have long been understood.[1] But it is remarkable how few critics have taken them into account, and how little scrutiny there has been, even in these days of close reading, of their precise implications in particular scenes or in particular relationships between characters.[2] I propose here to confine myself to an examination of what is conveyed by the use which Shakespeare makes of the *thou–you* distinction[3] in his portrayal of the relationship between Celia and Rosalind through the course of *As You Like It*.[4]

It should perhaps be noted that the conventions governing the choice of pronoun in English at that period – as indeed for a long time before – differed in an important respect from those which pertain in most European languages of the present day. For in earlier English, to a degree which does not seem to be paralleled elsewhere, the pronoun selected by a given speaker could in many circumstances vary from one moment to the next, even where that speaker is all the time addressing one and the same person. The selection is then often an 'expression of transient attitudes';[5] this is well illustrated by the shifts in which both Celia and Rosalind indulge.

Before embarking on details, I wish, at the risk of seeming trivial, to consider what is involved in a study of this kind. Our task is to restore as nearly as possible the old awareness of the effects conveyed by the selection of one as against the other form. I say 'effects' rather than 'effect' because an instance of, say, *thou* in one context will not necessarily have the same implication as an instance of it in another.[6] This task involves the close scrutiny, case by case, of the relevant pronouns, always within the framework of a fairly adequate (if sometimes over-rated) knowledge of Shakespeare's language as a whole. And for each instance we must postulate as the intended effect something which most convincingly fits in with all the other impressions conveyed to us by those numerous other touches which (unlike the *thou–you* distinction) are still capable today of making directly something of their original impact.

In the last resort, we may regard the whole text as a complex of such touches, though these will be of very different orders of significance and of subtlety and will also vary greatly in degree of amenability to analysis. Furthermore some will be more or less self-evident even to a modern reader, while others will not unless he can make some informed adjustment to earlier usage. But they may all have a bearing on the interpretation we seek to ascribe to instances of *thou* or *you*. In what follows I have not attempted except quite incidentally (cf. end-notes 10 and 12) to specify what it is about the text, linguistically or stylistically speaking, which has led me to the assumption of certain basic impressions as a background to such interpretations; this has been necessary in order to proceed at all within the scope of an article. But failure to specify implies no denial of the relevance of whatever I can learn from everything else in the text.

We naturally require, for any interpretation we may be tempted to make, some further support for it than that it seems to accord plausibly with the impressions we have from other touches. First, looking at our interpretations as a whole, we must assure ourselves that they form a workable and self-consistent system. We should certainly not reject the possibility of some system of considerable complexity, since both textual and extra-textual context[7] are always likely to produce significant variations of effect numerically far in excess of the basic two which one might, naïvely, expect from the operation of a two-term system like *thou–you*. At the same time we must not postulate an unbelievably complex set of effects, such that no contemporary of Shakespeare's could reasonably have been expected to find his way about in it, however admirably each of those we are tempted to postulate seems to us to fit a particular instance. And our means of control here must be to seek parallels elsewhere than in the text under immediate scrutiny for those effects we seek to justify. For it is not enough that the effect postulated in a given instance shall (at the least) do no violence to the impression made by all the other touches; it must also be an effect which squares with that suggested by any evidence which happens to be available about other instances of *thou* or *you* elsewhere which we judge to be relevantly similar in import. Again here, within the limits of this paper, I do not attempt to cite parallels. But I have not wittingly suggested any interpretation which I feel to be unjustifiable from this point of view.

We should not lose sight of one thing: that whatever we legitimately 'know' about Celia and Rosalind depends in the last resort on the text of *As You Like It* and our ability to interpret it. It is necessary to labour this point, because it is easy to fall into the delusion that we have some sort of non-textually derived acquaintance with such old friends. From here it is an easy step to a frame of mind where we refuse to allow any further evidence from the text (such as the demonstration of some hitherto unnoticed implication of a use of *thou*) to alter even in the slightest our ideas about the characters. And this is unfortunate, for we should always be prepared to go back to the text and re-examine it again and again without the drag of any such fixed ideas. Till we have caught in our text the whispered implication of every slightest linguistic nuance capable of yielding its import to us, our interpretation, however 'right' in a broad sort of way, must remain tentative.

A use of *thou* and *you* in Shakespeare is then a nuance to which we are trying to assign an import. And our procedure is to attempt to fit what is so far without any clear message to us into the pattern of those implications which the text *does* in various other ways succeed in putting across; it is a task of reconciliation, the conclusions from which must ultimately be verified in the ways I have already considered. But by 'reconciliation' it is not implied that such and such a use of the pronoun will necessarily achieve no more than the mere corroboration of an impression we have already picked up in full clarity from other things in the text. For every nuance is likely to make its own irreplaceable contribution. So we must be prepared to ask ourselves what, if anything, such a use *additionally* contributes. And if it does contribute something extra, we may find that this requires us to modify somewhat the interpretation of all the rest of the linguistic evidence from which we started. This kind of approach is familiar enough in lexicographical problems relating to past stages of the language.[8]

Our own problem is made the more difficult by the diversity of factors which may, in varying situations or relationships, as it were 'pull' a given speaker towards one or the other of the two modes. It is therefore easier to break into it in a preliminary way by choosing a set of cases where not all these complicating factors are present. It is partly for this reason that I have taken one where, though the situation of course changes, the same two persons are involved throughout. As I have already indicated, a full-scale attack on even this restricted problem would require that we hunt out many instances from elsewhere to support or corroborate the interpretation suggested for those under scrutiny. The present study attempts no more than to show the nature of the problem of interpretation and therefore, by implication, the kind of parallels which should be sought in a more comprehensive approach to the problem.

One may begin by observing that a certain atmosphere of relationship between Celia and Rosalind is quite clearly being built up by Shakespeare in the first scene where the two cousins are together [I ii]. If we examine the pronouns which they use in addressing one another here, we find something which (whatever else it may be) is statistically somewhat striking. For with two exceptions [lines 17, 254] Celia regularly uses the *thou* form, of which there are fifteen instances. Rosalind, on the other hand, uses the plural mode with only one exception [line 40]. She yields only five examples of *you*, but this is because of another touch: that she is much more quiet than Celia in this scene. Just what are we intended to catch from these pronominal uses?

I shall first consider Rosalind's addiction to *you*, since a general acquaintance with the conventions which governed Shakespeare's choice of pronoun at once suggests that this, in addressing a youthful girl cousin who is at the same time a close friend, is what is the more strongly in need of explanation. Rosalind is the daughter of the banished Duke; her position, as we are soon to find out, is insecure, and her status is to some degree inferior to that of Celia in the eyes of everyone except perhaps Celia herself. Rosalind is clearly aware of all this, and in normal circumstances (as here) she expresses her feelings by – among other things – a somewhat guarded protocol-observing and perhaps even slightly resentful *you*. We may at least say, I think, that her use of this pronoun strengthens and sharpens the impressions we pick up from all the other nuances in this scene.

Celia is in quite a different position. She is by nature impulsive and outgoing, she is at this time on top of the world, and she is in no way inhibited in her uncomplicated affection for Rosalind. We may say that her use of *thou* to Rosalind is in full accordance with these traits, and helps to adumbrate them. We may also suspect that the contrast of her *thou* with Rosalind's *you* should help to make us aware from the start of a certain uneasiness in their relationship.

In the English of the time a clear-cut convention such as we can observe in this scene may be expected to operate smoothly in what we may call 'normal rapport', but be broken if something happens to disturb the normality.[9] We may not always be able to explain a shift of pronominal mode, but we shall certainly be in a better position to do so once we have established what we can regard with some assurance as the conventions of normal rapport. Thereafter, in individual instances, we must always of course reckon, not only with textual error, but with the possibility that there may be situations where opposing tendencies result in there being at a given place no obviously 'right' and conversely 'wrong' form. Let us examine the deviations from the postulated norm in this introductory scene, and see what impression we can gain of their implications.

At line 17 Celia says:

You know my father hath no child but I, nor none is like to have; and truly, when he dies, thou shalt be his heir.

If anything is to be concluded from the pronominal modes here, it is that Celia opens with a momentary burst of impatience with Rosalind (foreshadowed in her previous speech) which she cannot sustain beyond the first fifteen words; thereafter she returns to, and for the present maintains, the sweeter kind of attitude 'conveyed' to us by the very first words she addresses to her cousin as the scene opens. The delivery of the following words [lines 18 ff.], beginning with the almost wheedling 'and, truly', is therefore intended to contrast sharply with what she has just said. The very quickness of the reversion to *thou* is itself a touch of some significance.

In line 254 Celia says:

> Will you go, coz?

This is spoken to Rosalind while she is loitering behind with Orlando in a somewhat unladylike manner. Celia has already (seven lines before) bidden formal farewell to Orlando, and now she is hanging about temporarily deserted by her beloved cousin in an unprecedented fashion. As in line 17, a certain annoyance, mingled this time perhaps with an ingredient of disquiet, would seem to be indicated by her shift to the plural mode; we shall hear more later of such bursts of annoyance and exasperation on Celia's part. We must also reckon (though I think this is less likely) with the possibility that the access of formality is prompted by nothing more than her having to address Rosalind in the presence of a stranger.

In lines 40 and following we have the only speech in this scene wherein Rosalind addresses Celia as *thou*:

> Nay, how thou goest from Fortune's office to Nature's: Fortune reigns in gifts of the world, not in the lineaments of Nature.

Here it may be that the preceding fantasy of Celia's, which she has pursued to try to cheer Rosalind, has at last had the effect of jogging her, for the moment at least, out of her more reserved and guarded attitude. But I would stress that such suggested explanations as I here offer are mere first approximations. Such hypotheses must stand or fall according to the findings of a much wider scrutiny of related instances; I am merely sketching part of a frame of reference for a much more exhaustive study which is long overdue.

There is further dialogue between Celia and Rosalind in the next scene [I iii]. Here Rosalind uses the plural mode regularly, though since (as usual at this stage of the play) she is for most of the scene both more silent and also more impersonal[10] than Celia, we have only four instances. Celia uses the second person pronoun no less than 27 times. She uses *thou* 17 times, *you* 10 times, and she makes eight shifts. This can be made clear in a table:

C sg.	4		13 21				89	90(2)	91(2)	92	93(2)	96(2)
pl.		10		24(2)	27	31						
C sg.				104(2)		122(2)						
pl.	101(2)	102(2)			112							

This contrasts remarkably both with the regularity of her use of *thou* in the previous scene and with Rosalind's still stable pronominal habits. And since we are regarding Celia's *thou* as her pronoun of normal rapport with Rosalind, it is her employment of *you* in this scene which requires special examination.

We should perhaps consider the first five instances separately, for these all come before the disrupting moment when Frederick orders Rosalind to leave the court. Up to this point Celia and Rosalind would at first sight seem to be in much the same sort of situation as in the previous scene; yet something must have happened. My own impression is that all these first cases of *you* carry once more an overtone of disquiet and annoyance, this time an annoyance related directly to Rosalind's preoccupation with Orlando. This is foreshadowed at the end of the previous scene, but the situation *has* in fact changed in that it is increasingly more clear to Celia that she has a rival to her own affections. One need not pursue the point here, but it may be suggested that this reaction of Celia's is the stronger because she seems from the beginning to be in greater need of Rosalind's affection than Rosalind of hers. And so it is only intermittently now that Celia can overcome her feelings about this and treat her cousin in quite the old carefree way. There will be more to say about this when we come to Act III, scene ii.

The remaining cases [in I iii] occur in lines 101–2 and 112:

Therefore devise with me how we may fly,
Whither to go, and what to bear with us:
And do not seek to take your change upon you
To bear your griefs yourself and leave me out:
For, by this heaven, now at our sorrows pale,
Say what thou canst, I'll go along with thee.   [99–104]

I'll put myself in poor and mean attire,
And with a kind of umber smirch my face;
The like do you: so shall we pass along
And never stir assailants.   [110–13]

It may be suggested that lines 112–13 represent a short burst of anxious petulance, an impulsive taking of offence at the mere thought of Rosalind perhaps having it in mind to go off without her. But (rather as in the shift between lines 17 and 18 of Act I, scene ii) Celia cannot sustain this mood and she modulates into an expression of devoted and dependent loyalty in the following two lines. As in the earlier instance, the selection of *you* and then of *thou* is, on this interpretation, a sort of key to the contrasting tone in which the first and second pairs of these last four lines should be delivered. As for line 112, I can suggest no very convincing interpretation; it is one of the rare cases where the pronoun selected is not accounted for by the present suggestions.[11]

The next relevant scene is III ii [lines 156 ff.]. Here we have a quite remarkable change, for *both* girls now depart from the pronominal conventions which characterised their normal rapport, and over a large stretch of text [lines 180 ff.] their modes are completely reversed. As before, what happens can be shown in tabular form:

	NORMAL		REVERSED						
R pl. C sg.	156(2) 163 172 173	176							
R sg. C pl.			180 182 183	184	190 195 198 199 200 201				

	REVERSED (*continued*)	NORMAL	REVERSED
R pl C sg.		251 245(2) 249	
R sg. C pl.	203(2) 204 212 221 224 225 205(2) 226		253

This patterning is clearly no accident, however tentative any detailed explanation of it may have to be. Were it not that the opening part of the scene (up to line 179) displays their conventions of normal rapport, one might suppose that this of itself had once and for all shifted with the now radically different circumstances and relationship in which the two girls find themselves. But as things are this can hardly be the case.

The change, which is initiated by Celia, does not come till line 180:

> ROSALIND. I was seven of the nine days out of the wonder before you came; for look here what I found on a palm-tree; I was never so be-rimed since Pythagoras' time, that I was an Irish rat, which I can hardly remember.
> CELIA. Trow you who hath done this? [III ii 175–80]

Hereafter we have an uninterrupted run of twenty instances of a reversal of their normal modes. So far as Celia is concerned, it is difficult not to connect this with something we have already noticed. Once more she is faced with the intrusion of Orlando into the cosiness of their hitherto undisturbed relationship and, as this becomes more and more of a menace, it more and more clearly introduces a note of huffiness into Celia's attitude and an element of estrangement foreign to her side of the original relationship. I have suggested that this is probably foreshadowed earlier [I ii 254; I iii 10 and 24–31].

Rosalind's reversal here must be related to the excited state of mind induced by Orlando. Her normal reserve breaks down: she is unprecedently loquacious, and she will now go to all lengths of girlish directness and unreserve to clarify her uncertainties, cf. 203–4:

> I prithee, take the cork out of thy mouth, that I may drink thy tidings.

This shift to *thou* from line 184 onwards contributes in its small

way to the throwing of the main emotional interest now quite
sharply on to Rosalind herself; she is more and more clearly
revealed as being transformed by love. And, caparison'd like a
man as she now is, the dramatic effect of this is the more
telling.[12]

If this interpretation is more or less on the right lines, we are
left with the problem of the reversion to the old pattern
between lines 245 and 251. Again it is Celia who initiates it,
this time (it would seem) rather in the mood of an impetuous
child. Up to line 239 ('give me audience, good madam') she
has, whether satirically or otherwise, been observing a certain
distance and formality. But at line 254 she breaks down:

Cry 'holla!' to thy tongue, I prithee; its curvets unseasonably.

In similar vein she says at line 249:

I would sing my song without a burthen: thou bringest me out of tune.

And when Rosalind replies [lines 251], it is in a mood of calm
more like her old self, but tinged now with a new touch of
superiority:

Do you not know I am a woman? when I think, I must speak. Sweet, say on.

Celia's final reply here [line 253] is in the plural mode:

You bring me out. Soft! comes he not here?

The first four words are an aposiopesis,[13] echoing her previous
'thou bringest me out of tune', but this time reflecting a huffier
and more distant frame of mind probably directly brought on
by Rosalind's rather patronising previous words.

The next scene in which the cousins converse [III iv] tells us
little: there are only three relevant instances of pronouns, a
singular by Celia (line 2) and two plurals by Rosalind [lines
22, 28].[14] Rosalind is no longer keyed up, and her reversion to
the plural mode seems appropriate enough here. So also does
Celia's single *prithee*; I suspect however that if Celia had had
occasion to use any second person pronouns after line 8 or
thereabouts, they would have been plurals, to reinforce the
impression of her exasperation.

In Act IV, scene i we have another upset of the mode of

normal rapport; the instances are not numerous, but there are no exceptions and the passage is of considerable interest:

C p.	96(2) 197 198		204	
R sg.			201	210

Here, more clearly than in the middle of Act III, scene ii, one has corroboration from other touches that Celia is voicing a certain feeling of estrangement from this disquieting new cousin of hers. In lines 196 and following [IV i], this implication of the *you*'s is in strict keeping with the whole tenor of what she says:

> You have simply misused our sex in your love-prate: we must have your doublet and hose plucked over your head, and show the world what the bird hath done to her own nest.

And Celia's sense of deprivation is offset now by still clearer signs than hitherto of a new superiority on Rosalind's side of the relationship [line 200]:

> O coz, coz, coz, my pretty little coz, that thou didst know how many fathom deep I am in love.

This is the last scene in which the two girls have any intimate exchanges. When they appear in Act IV, scene iii, they are for a brief moment alone [lines 1–5] and they both use *you* once [lines 1, 3]; no comment of much value can be offered on so short a passage. Thereafter all we have is three more plural forms from Celia [lines 161, 176(2)]. But this is Aliena speaking to Ganymede in the presence of others, and this is probably in keeping with the public conventions of their rapport in this artificial role.[15] It is interesting that thereafter, throughout the whole of Act V, they never exchange another word. So from III iv onward there is a steady toning down of their friendship; as we move through the latter part of the play, the girlish intimacy, never indeed completely secure and balanced, yet so much to the fore in the beginning, recedes into the background. For we are being prepared for Hymen and the honouring of high wedlock and the old relationship has had its day.

SOURCE: article in *A Review of English Literature*, IV, 2 (1963), pp. 68–81; reprinted with revisions in A. McIntosh and M. A. K. Halliday, *Patterns of Language* (1966).

NOTES

[Reorganised and renumbered from the original – Ed.]

1. See esp. A. E. Abbott, *Shakespearean Grammar* (2nd edn, 1870), para. 232ff.; and W. Franz, *Shakespeare-Grammatik* (Heidelberg, 1924), para. 289ff. References to a number of works on various aspects of this opposition in different European languages will be found in R. Brown and A. Gilman, 'The Pronouns of Power and Solidarity', in Thomas A. Sebeok, *Style in Language* (New York and London, 1960), p. 253. Among these, particular mention may be made of Sister St G. Byrne, *Shakespeare's Use of the Pronouns of Address* (dissertation, Catholic University of America, Washington, 1936). For Middle English, see also W. W. Skeat, *William of Palerne* (Early English Text Society, ES No. 1, 1867), pp. *xli–xliii*. *Additional Note*: A valuable analysis of Shakespeare's use of *thou* and *you* is made in an unpublished dissertation: Raymond Adlam, '*Thou* and *You*: Some Pronominal Shifts in Shakespeare' (for the Diploma in Applied Linguistics, University of Edinburgh, 1964). For a general survey, see also T. Finkenstaedt, 'You' and 'Thou': *Studien zur Anrede im Englischen* (Berlin 1963). For a discussion of the use of the two pronouns in *Sir Gawain and the Green Knight*, see the edition of Israel Gollancz (EETS, OS 210), note to line 1071. Further references are given by Norman Davies, 'The *Litera Troili* and English Letters', *Review of English Studies*, NS, XVI, No. 63 (1965), p. 243, footnote 5. [Recent work in this field includes G. L. Brook, *The Language of Shakespeare* (1976), and relevant material in the symposium, *Shakespeare's Styles* (1980), excerpted below (see p. 130). Sister Miriam Joseph's Shakespeare's *Use of the Arts of Language* (1947) remains of great value – Ed.]

2. Cf. A. McIntosh and C. F. Williamson, '*King Lear*, Act I, Scene i: Two Stylistic Notes', *Review of English Studies* (1962), NS, XIV, No. 53 (1963), p. 54.

3. I am, of course, considering *you* in its *singular use*. In speaking of *thou* and *you*, I imply all related forms: *thy, thine, your* etc. For convenience, I shall sometimes refer to uses involving the *th*-forms as uses of the singular mode, those involving *y*-forms as of the plural mode.

4. Line references are to the edition of the play in *The Comedies of Shakespeare* (Oxford, 1922). The passages which concern us are in I ii; I iii; III ii; III iv; III v; IV i; and IV iii. I have noted 105 relevant second-person pronouns in them; eight of these are used by Aliena and Ganymede when speaking in public: cf. note 15, below.

5. See Brown and Gilman, op. cit. (note 1, above), pp. 253–4, 273–6. *Additional Note*: Professor E. Lapesa, University of Madrid, has advised me (in private conversation) that similar shifts occur in Classical Spanish; there are for instance striking examples in *Don Quixote*.

6. Cf. note 9, below. In the technical sense I attach to the word *use*, I should speak of two such instances exemplifying two different uses.

7. By these terms I mean 'what occurs in the passage under examination', and 'what occurs outside that particular passage'.

8. It may be noted that many more straightforward and typical lexical problems than that of *thou* and *you* await a similar sort of delicate analysis in Shakespeare. Who at present, for instance, could with any assurance give a full account of the various implications of Shakespeare's uses of *accommodate* and *accommodation*? For a discussion of *one* instance of *accommodate* [*King Lear*, IV vi 82], see Hilda M. Hulme, *Explorations in Shakespeare's Language* (1962), pp. 275–7.

9. It would doubtless not always be easy to define 'normal rapport', but there are numerous cases throughout Shakespeare where we can establish it without difficulty. Thus, it is normal in *Twelfth Night* for Sir Toby to address Sir Andrew as *thou*, and for the latter to address the former as *you*. It is instructive to note (however obvious this may be) that the motivation of these uses by Sir Toby and Sir Andrew is very different from that of Celia and Rosalind, though not totally so.

10. By 'impersonal', I mean that, up to a certain point in the play, whenever Rosalind speaks she tends much less to involve Celia directly than Celia does when speaking to her. Apart from the use of second-person pronouns, the main markers which indicate such involvement of the hearers are: (1) The use of *we, us, our*, etc.; (2) vocatives; (3) questions; (4) imperatives. Note that Rosalind's use of a mere five instances of these markers in I iii 1–104 is by no means fully explained by her taciturnity. For Celia uses well over four times as many as Rosalind does for each hundred words spoken. It should be observed that the whole pattern changes about line 105, where Rosalind's interest in a joint flight begins to quicken. Hereafter in the scene she not only speaks more than Celia, but in what she says there is now a far heavier incidence than before of these markers of involvement. For instance, three of the four second-person pronouns that she uses in this scene come in this short passage. Even here, however, Rosalind's 'score' still falls well below Celia's remarkable average (over the whole scene) of one marker or another to every six words she utters. The pattern at its two stages in I iii may be demonstrated in tabular fashion:

	lines 1–104		lines 105–137	
	Rosalind	Celia	Rosalind	Celia
thou, you, etc.	1	24	3	3
we, us, etc.	0	6	6	6
vocatives	0	7	1	0
questions	0	12	5	1
imperatives	4	7	1	4
Totals	5	56	16	14
Total number of words spoken	124	303	142	117

For a marked change in the ways in which (in a subsequent scene) Rosalind involves Celia, see note 12, below. *Additional Note*: I touch on this question of involvement in 'Language and Style', *Durham University Journal* (June 1963), pp. 120–1. For an even more striking case of imbalance in the involvement-relation between two characters, see *Macbeth*, II ii 22–58 & 65–73.

11. It should be added that there may be circumstances where the choice of forms is affected by grammatical or lexical factors. Abbott (op. cit., para. 234) touches on something of this sort (not relevant to the instance here in our discussion): namely, that *you* may be used in conditional and other sentences where there is no direct appeal to the person addressed in situations where *thou* would be used in statements and requests. Franz (op. cit.), however, makes no allusion to any such conditioning. *Additional Note*: Since the above was written, Raymond Adlam has discovered that Abbott's conjecture is erroneous, being based either on passages which are corrupt or (in one case) on a conflation of an 18th-century text.

12. It is worth presenting for III ii an 'involvement table' similar to that which relates to I iii (cf. note 10):

	lines 180–254	
	Rosalind	Celia
thou, you, etc.	15	11
vocatives	3	1
we, us, etc.	0	0
questions	22	4
imperatives	11	5
Totals	51	21
Total number of words spoken	310	228

We may note that the incidence of second-person pronouns is now about equal, but there is no more talk of *we* and *us*. Questions and imperatives now fall heavily on Rosalind's side. This is clearly a new kind of involvement, very different from that in I iii 105–37.

13. [Ed.] *Aposiopesis*: a speaker's halting mid-way in a sentence, either through excitement or other emotional disturbance, or with a desire to hint at things inexpressible.

14. The *your* of Celia at III iv 12 is not, of course, relevant.

15. We know, at any rate, that Ganymede always uses *you* to Aliena in such cases: cf. III v 75; IV i 118, 119, 123; IV iii 66.

Stanley Wells 'The Nurse's Speeches in *Romeo and Juliet*: I iii' (1980)

The style of the Nurse's speeches in Act I, scene iii of *Romeo and Juliet* makes a vivid impact on both readers and spectators. It is described by Nicholas Brooke as 'something altogether new, both in this play and, in fact, in Shakespeare's output'. He finds its 'nearest antecedent', not in verse, but in 'the prose of I i'. While 'it goes far beyond that', nevertheless 'its characteristic is that it is close to prose, or rather to prosaic speech, developing its own rhythmic momentum'.[1] By the time that Shakespeare wrote *Romeo and Juliet* he had written much dialogue that approximates to prosaic speech rather than to literary prose; and I should like to begin this essay by examining some of the characteristics of the Nurse's utterance which may account for the claim that it represents 'something altogether new'.

It is easy to point to aspects of the style which create the illusion of spontaneity. There are colloquial expressions such as 'Come Lammas Eve at night'; 'Shake, quoth the dovehouse' (so personal as to be obscure in meaning); 'stand high-lone'; and 'broke her brow'. The diction is familiar, even vulgar: 'dug', 'tetchy', 'trudge', 'waddled'. There are emphatic or asseverative expressions, including: 'Well'; 'as I said'; 'marry'; 'Nay'; 'I trow'; 'by th'rood'; 'by my holidam'; 'I warrant'. Some of these words and phrases, and others, are repeated or slightly varied in a manner that would be avoided by a literary artist but which helps to bind the speech together and to give the impression that they are idiosyncratic to the speaker: 'God rest all Christian souls!' . . . 'God be with his soul!': is this sententiousness or piety? – the performer may decide; 'I remember it well . . . I never shall forget it . . . I never should forget it'; 'pretty fool . . . pretty wretch . . . pretty fool'; and 'To see it . . . To see, now. . .'.

These devices might equally well be discerned in the racy prose dialogue of Act I, scene i, or in individually longer prose speeches, such as Launce's principal soliloquies in *The Two Gentlemen of Verona* [II iii; IV iv]. More individual to the Nurse is the structure and argument of the speech (or, in effect, its denial of structure and argument): the sequence of ideas and images, and the aim to which they are applied. Coleridge referred to them in an 'Essay on Method in Thought'[2] as an example of Shakespeare's exhibitions of 'the difference between the products of a well disciplined and those of an uncultivated understanding'. He remarks that 'the absence of Method, what characterises the uneducated, is occasioned by a habitual submission of the understanding to mere events and images as such, and independent of any power in the mind to classify or appropriate them'. One very obvious symptom of the 'absence of Method' in the Nurse's disquisition is the frequency with which she interrupts herself. Sometimes this is because she follows an associative train of thought irrespective of its relevance to her listeners:

> I'll lay fourteen of my teeth –
> And yet, to my teen be it spoken, I have but four –
> She's not fourteen.

Is her self-interruption here a conscious playing with 'four' and 'teen', or rather the subconscious struggle to clear her mind of verbal entanglements? Again, the performer may choose.

Part of the comedy of the Nurse's utterance lies in the fact that what she interrupts has in itself no logical sequence. The information that she has to convey in her main speech is entirely contained in its second line:

> Come Lammas Eve at night shall she be fourteen.

This fact might well be pointed by stage business, Lady Capulet endeavouring to resume the conversation after this statement. But the Nurse's well of recollection has been tapped, and the flow cannot be quenched. Coleridge parallels this speech of the Nurse with one of Mistress Quickly. In answer to Falstaff's question 'What is the gross sum that I owe thee?', she replies

Marry, if thou wert an honest man, thyself and the money too. Thou didst swear to me upon a parcel-gilt goblet, sitting in my Dolphin chamber, at the round table, by a sea-coal fire, upon Wednesday in Wheeson week, when the Prince broke thy head for liking his father to a singing-man of Windsor – thou didst swear to me then, as I was washing thy wound, to marry me and make me my lady thy wife. Canst thou deny it? Did not goodwife Keech, the butcher's wife, come in then and call me gossip Quickly? Coming in to borrow a mess of vinegar, telling us she had a good dish of prawns, whereby thou didst desire to eat some, whereby I told thee they were ill for a green wound? [*2 Henry IV*, II i 81–94]

Here, Coleridge remarks that 'the connexions and sequence which the habit of Method can alone give have in this instance a substitute in the fusion of passion'. The Nurse lacks Mistress Quickly's vituperative passion of self-righteous indignation, but her recollections, too, are grounded in emotion, provoked by the memory that she had had a daughter of the same age as Juliet. The very fact that Susan's relationship with the Nurse is not explicitly stated is itself an aspect of Shakespeare's dramatic style here. It tells us obliquely of the Nurse's intimacy with the family in which she lives: an intimacy which the performers can use by suggesting a sympathetic, if bored, acceptance that once the Nurse has embarked on this tack, she must be indulged. And it engages the audience by requiring them to make the inference. The death of an infant has an inevitable poignancy, and one which must link the Nurse to the Capulets since Juliet has thriven on the milk which should have reared Susan. And we may recall that the shadow of infant mortality has already darkened the play, in Capulet's 'Earth hath swallowed all my hopes but she' [I ii 14].

The Nurse's recollection that Juliet and Susan 'Were of an age' is interrupted by the pious commonplace 'God rest all Christian souls!', leading us to infer that Susan is dead, and is followed by two more clichés: 'Susan is with God;/She was too good for me.' The ordinariness of these expressions is surely part of their point; they come naturally from the mouth of a simple-minded woman. To say, as G. I. Duthie does in the New Cambridge edition,[3] 'She knows she has faults. When she declares that little Susan was too good for her, she is speaking partly jocularly but partly, for a second, seriously, with self-knowledge', is surely to ignore the stereotyped quality of the assertion.

After her digression, the Nurse's pulling herself up with 'But, as I said', and coming full circle with

> On Lammas Eve at night shall she be fourteen,

marks another point at which she might have concluded. But her recollections have a self-generating momentum, and as she goes on, she becomes increasingly self-absorbed. Coleridge's 'Method' implies consideration for the listener (or reader), an ordering of statements requiring the application of fundamental brainwork such as is associated with literary artistry or conscious rhetoric, and is thus outward-looking. The 'absence of Method', on the other hand, implies a delving into the subconscious which produces the kind of monologue that achieves communication rather by accident than by design. The Nurse makes no pretence that her ramblings are relevant to the situation. They are a form of self-indulgence which is also a form of both self-investigation and (when conducted in public) self-revelation, so the response of listeners is a measure of their response to the speaker's character. The Nurse's listeners allow her to continue; whether they do so with complete indulgence or with some degree of indifference, and with attempts to interrupt, is open to interpretation. The Nurse's repetitions of 'But, as I said' may be regarded as a method of staving off interruption, or they may be less outward-looking, her own method of attempting to exert some control over her discourse.

After concluding the first paragraph of her speech, she marks time for a moment with 'That shall she, marry; I remember it well' before embarking on another paragraph whose beginning also is to reappear as its ending. And from the recollection of one landmark – Lammas Eve as the time of the infant's birth – she passes to another: the day of 'the earthquake' as that on which Juliet was weaned. That Shakespeare was here considerately making a topical allusion in order to help scholars of the future to know when he wrote his play is improbable. An 'earthquake' is chosen as the kind of event which would be significant in the lives of all who experienced it, an episode certain to engrave itself upon the collective memory. It serves again to link the masters with their servants. The coincidence of Juliet's being weaned on the day of the earthquake is stressed in the phrase 'Of all the days of the year', and seems to confer importance upon the event; but always, as these facts emerge, they are linked and given significance by being shown as part of the life-experience of the woman who recollects them. It is her memory in which they dwell – 'I remember it well', 'I never shall forget it'; and it is her body with which they are associated.

So far we have had only statements; now, as she becomes more immersed in her topic, she becomes anecdotal. The absence of intellectual logic in what she says is apparent in the false connective 'For' – 'For I had then laid wormwood to my dug' – but the sudden sequence of nouns in this and the succeeding line – 'wormwood . . . dug . . . sun . . . dovehouse' and 'wall' – helps to create a vivid picture of peaceful normality which gains in credibility by its association with a violently abnormal event. Yet another association obtrudes – 'My lord and you were then at Mantua' – and the pressure of recollection becomes so great that the Nurse returns to the present in wonderment at her own mental powers – 'Nay, I do bear a brain.'[4]

She resumes her anecdote, losing herself again in memories which allow no acknowledgement that the baby of whom she speaks is the girl who stands beside her. Her style is not expository but exclamatory, deepening the suggestion that she is re-living the experience:

> pretty fool,
> To see it tetchy, and fall out with the dug!

This exclamation is followed by another, elliptical and slightly obscure,[5] which recalls the earthquake's shocking disruption of normality – 'Shake, quoth the dovehouse.' Again she is jolted back to the present as she recalls her hasty flight and rounds off the second paragraph with a return to the statement with which it began: 'And since that time it is eleven years.'

The final part of the speech again begins with a false connective, and has no logical link with what precedes it, nor even any obvious associative one, unless it is that the Nurse's memory of her need to 'trudge'[6] leads from her own legs to Juliet's, and thus to the recollection that Juliet was able to *stand* by herself. The second anecdote features another newly introduced character, the Nurse's husband; the touch of sadness that he is dead is offset by her memory of him as 'a merry man'. For the first time now she quotes direct speech, in her husband's somewhat bawdy, familiar remark to the child 'Jule'. The Nurse's own, self-absorbed delight in her recollections is evident in her repetition of the anecdote. Whether she has carried her stage audience along with her is again a matter for interpretation. Lady Capulet's interruption,

> Enough of this. I pray thee, hold thy peace

appears to demonstrate impatience, yet it can be played against its sense, in full enjoyment of the comedy of the tale. Coleridge referred to the Nurse's 'childlike fondness of repetition in her childish age – and that happy, humble ducking under, yet resurgence against the check –

> Yes, madam! *Yet* I cannot choose but laugh.'[7]

And she adds the circumstantial and bawdy detail of the 'bump as big as a young cock'rel's stone' before winding herself to a standstill with her fourth telling of the tale.

I have written of the speech so far as if it were composed in prose, not verse. I have referred to the 'prose' characteristics of its diction and structure, and to the fact that it quotes a passage of (supposedly) prose speech. Although in modern editions we read the speech as verse, it is a curious fact that it was printed as prose in all the early editions: the bad quarto (1597), the good quarto (1599), and the First Folio (1623). It is less surprising that verse should appear as prose in the memorially reconstructed bad quarto than that most of the Nurse's speeches in this scene are set in italic type in both quartos. There is evidence that in Q2 the first thirty-four lines of the scene are reprinted directly from Q1,[8] and it is likely that this fact influenced the Q2 compositor to go on setting these speeches as prose even though they were presumably written out as verse in the holograph from which he is believed to have set the remainder of the scene. Not until Capell's edition (1768) were the Nurse's speeches arranged as verse. In the meantime Thomas Otway had adapted and amplified them, while retaining their substance, in unmistakable prose in his *Caius Marius* (1679). Garrick, naturally, set them as prose in his adaptation of 1748, followed, in spite of Capell, in John Bell's acting edition (1774). At least two nineteenth-century editors – Staunton (1857) and Keightley (1865) – did the same, and so does Frank A. Marshall in the *Henry Irving Shakespeare* (8 vols, 1888–90), with a note condemning 'the modern editors who have tried to make verse of what was surely never intended for it', and asking: 'Why should Shakespeare be made to violate every rule of rhythm and metre, for the sake of trying to strain this conventional prose into blank verse?' (vol. I, p. 240). Irving's acting edition of 1882, however, prints the expurgated remnants as verse.[9] G. B. Harrison reverted to prose in his Penguin edition (1937), and even Dover Wilson wrote that 'editors have never been able to make anything but very rough verse out of these speeches and it is quite possible that Shakespeare intended them to be rhythmical (i.e. easily memorised) prose'.[10] But this statement is impressionistic rather than accurate. G. Walton Williams (p. 107) analyses the scene carefully and shows that the earlier section of the Nurse's long speech 'is marked by irregular verse': the nineteen lines include one four-syllable line [35], three hypermetrical lines with unaccented final syllables [18, 22, 31]; and five hypermetrical lines with accented final syllables [23, 25, 26, 28 and 32]. These are not violent irregularities, and several of them may be explained as contractions in pronunciation; the remainder of the scene, Williams finds, is 'in smooth verse' with minor exceptions. Minor rhythmic irregularities may be expected in verse which is so clearly intended as this is to represent 'prosaic speech'. As Kenneth Muir says: 'Shakespeare obtains some subtle effects by the verse rhythm underlying the apparently colloquial speech.'[11] Little more than a glance is needed to show that in both the inauthentically and the authentically derived sections, the ends of lines are almost invariably also the ends of sense-units: the only enjambment in the main speech is at lines 31–2 ('the nipple / Of my dug . . .'). There can be no question that Shakespeare was fully conscious that he was writing verse, nor, to my mind, that he was going further than ever before in the experiment of combining the diction, rhythms, and even mental processes normally associated with prose utterance within the over-all rhythms of blank verse. The speeches would be remarkable enough as an exhibition of the 'quick forge and working-house of thought' if they had indeed been in prose; it is the fact that in them prose rhythms are counterpointed against a verse structure that makes them 'something altogether new, both in this play and . . . in Shakespeare's output'. . . .

SOURCE: extract from 'Juliet's Nurse: The Uses of Inconsequentiality', in P. Edwards, I.–S. Ewbank and G. K. Hunter (eds), *Shakespeare's Styles: Essays in Honour of Kenneth Muir* (Cambridge, 1980), pp. 52–8.

NOTES

[Reorganised from the original – Ed.]

1. N. Brooke, *Shakespeare's Early Tragedies* (London, 1968), p. 92.
2. Coleridge, in *The Friend* (1818); reproduced in T. Hawkes (ed.), *Coleridge on Shakespeare*, Penguin Shakespeare Library (Harmondsworth, 1969), pp. 87–8.
3. G. I. Duthie (ed.), *Romeo and Juliet*, New Cambridge Edition (Cambridge, 1955), p. *xxxvi*.
4. There is ample evidence that this phrase, recorded as a proverb – cf. M. P. Tilley, *A Dictionary of the Proverbs in England in the Sixteenth and Seventeenth Centuries* (Ann Arbor, 1950), B 596 – is self-gratulatory, meaning (as Isaac Reed glossed it): 'I have a perfect remembrance or recollection'. The opposite meaning, however, may readily suggest itself to a modern reader, resulting in George Skillan's note, in French's Acting Edition of the play (London, 1947): 'then suddenly realising that she is getting somewhat away from her subject and admitting it'. T. J. B. Spencer seems to concede some doubt in his gloss – New Penguin Edition (Harmondsworth, 1967) – '(perhaps) I have a good memory still'.
5. Barbara Everett – in her subtle essay, '*Romeo and Juliet*: The Nurse's Story', *Critical Quarterly* (Summer, 1972), pp. 129–39 – writes that '''Shake,

quoth the dovehouse", has not been helpfully enough glossed, presumably because few Shakespeare editors are sufficiently acquainted with what might be said to a very small child about an earthquake. It does not simply mean, as has been suggested, "the dovehouse shook"; it allows the unfluttered dovecote to satirise the earthquake, as in a comical baby mock-heroic -- to be aloof and detached from what is happening to it' (p. 135).

6. I take it that the Nurse is saying that she was so shaken by the earthquake that she 'trudged' without having to be told to do so. Barbara Everett's comments on the passage (op. cit., p. 146) seem rather to imply that the Nurse is saying that Juliet, in her tetchiness, had no call to send the Nurse packing, that the dovehouse was unimpressed equally by the fury of the earthquake and by the infant's crossness, and (possibly) that the Nurse was no more impressed by either. This seems to me to be an equally acceptable interpretation.

7. *Coleridge on Shakespeare*, op. cit., p. 135.

8. See G. Walton Williams (ed.), *William Shakespeare: The Most Excellent and Lamentable Tragedie of Romeo and Juliet -- A Critical Edition* (Durham, N. C., 1964), p. *xii*.

9. It is of only incidental interest that the published screen-script of Metro-Goldwyn-Mayer's film, starring Norma Shearer and Leslie Howard, prints *all* the verse as prose, with the explanation that this helped the actors 'to speak the lines as Hamlet wished his players to speak theirs, "trippingly on the tongue"' -- *A Motion Picture Version of Shakespeare's 'Romeo and Juliet'* (New York, 1936), p. 249.

10. J. Dover Wilson, 'The New Way with Shakespeare's Text', *Shakespeare Survey*, 8 (Cambridge, 1955), p. 98.

11. Kenneth Muir, *Shakespeare's Tragic Sequence* (London, 1972), p. 40.

F. W. Bateson   'Denotative and Connotative Language in Metaphysical Poetry' (1934)

. . . The condition of the English language in the first half of the seventeenth century was especially favourable to poetic ambiguities. A language, considered semantically, evolves by a series of conflicts between the denotative and the connotative forces in words -- between 'an asceticism tending to kill language by stripping words of all association and a hedonism tending to kill language by dissipating their sense under a multiplicity of associations'.[1] The seventeenth century in England, from this point of view, was predominantly a connotative period. It was an epoch, linguistically as well as politically, of expansion. New words were being coined or borrowed all the time, and the tendencies that made for the introduction of new words were also active in adding new shades of meaning and new areas of context (a breeding-ground for the poetic ambiguity) in words already in use. (Thomas Carew actually associates 'the juggling feat of two-edged words' with 'whatsoever wrong By ours was done the Greek or Latin tongue'.[2]) The process was sometimes carried so far that the primary senses of words almost disappear in their derived meanings and associations. The phrases of Shakespeare and Donne, in particular, often seem to be on the point of sloughing their original meanings and vanishing, bright winged things, in the aura of suggestion they irradiate. Consider, for example, their use of the word *brave*:

> How beauteous mankind is! O brave new world,
> That has such people in't.

> I have done one braver thing
>   Than all the Worthies did.

The word hovers between its normal meanings of 'courageous' and 'finely-dressed' and transcends them. Miranda's *new world* is not so much beautiful as exciting and romantic, a promised land of colour and adventure in which Right will always be Might; and similarly Donne's *braver thing* – to 'forget the He and She' – is not essentially an act of courage but of grace, a chivalrous gesture of the Platonic knight. Herrick's 'Infanta' is another and a more tangible example of the same process:

> Aske me why I send you here
> This sweet Infanta of the yeere?

The dictionary defines 'Infanta' as a 'daughter of the King and Queen of Spain or Portugal, especially the eldest daughter who is not heir to the throne'. That is what 'Infanta' denotes. What it connotes, which was all Herrick was interested in, is an infant who is also an exotic princess. Herrick had no intention of *comparing* his primrose to the eldest daughter of the King of Spain. That would be to read a logical precision into his words that they do not possess, and the possession of which would have been fatal to the vague splendour of his poem.

The ambiguity and the use of words simply for their associative values are particular instances of a more general characteristic of the metaphysical style: its tendency to push words a little beyond their normal meanings. The peculiar vividness of metaphysical poetry is primarily due to the almost imperceptible twist – a 'perpetual slight alteration of language, words perpetually juxtaposed in new and sudden combinations, meanings perpetually *eingeschachtelt* into meanings'[3] – that by the unexpected collocations of words and phrases it succeeded in giving to language:

> Why does yon fellow falsify highways,
> And lays his life between the judge's lips
> To refine such a one? Keeps horse and men
> To beat their valours for her?[4]

> Let the priest in surplice white,
> That defunctive music can,
> Be the death-divining swan.[5]

Falsify highways, beat their valours, defunctive music – such phrases are of the essence of metaphysical poetry. They could only have been coined in these sixty wonderful years, the Golden Age of English poetry, between 1590 and 1650, and they were only made possible by the peculiar vitality and elasticity of the language of the period. But the device, for all its brilliant success, was fundamentally an abuse of language. A language is a vehicle of communication, or it is nothing. The metaphysical writers by continually extending the common meanings of words – the vividness they required was only obtainable so – gradually cut the ground away from under themselves. Their innovations, if they were to be innovations and not repetitions, had to be progressively more and more audacious and less and less intelligible. And it became impossible finally to say a plain thing in a plain way. The *impasse* is already evident in Shakespeare's *Henry VIII*:

> men might say,
> Till this time, pomp was single, but now married
> To one above itself. Each following day
> Became the next day's master, till the last
> Made former wonders its.

A style so tortuous and cumbrous, however capable it might be of momentary flashes of beauty, was no longer adequate as a medium of communication. . . .

SOURCE: extract from *English Poetry and the English Language* (Oxford, 1934; 2nd edition, 1961), pp. 43–6.

NOTES

[Reorganised and renumbered from the original – Ed.]

1. *Oxford Poetry* (Oxford, 1927): one of a series of anthologies published from 1913 onward by Basil Blackwell and Co.
2. Thomas Carew, 'An Elegy upon the Death of Dr Donne'.
3. T. S. Eliot, essay on Philip Massinger, in *The Sacred Wood* (1920), p. 117; reproduced in *Selected Essays* (London, 1932, 3rd edition, 1951), p. 209.
4. Tourneur, *The Revenger's Tragedy* [III i].
5. Shakespeare, 'The Phoenix and the Turtle'.

Francis Berry   'Argument by Mood in Marvell's *To his Coy Mistress*' (1958)

. . . A total of forty-six lines, in three paragraphs, go to make up Marvell's *To his Coy Mistress*. Of these forty-six lines the first paragraph claims as many as twenty. (The second has twelve, the third fourteen.) Now it should be understood that the whole of this first paragraph – with the exception of the nineteenth line, which states a fact, namely:

For Lady you deserve this State;

– is a deliberate exercise within the limits of the subjunctive. Within the limits? But that is a paradox, because in the subjunctive realms, unlike the indicative world which is inexorably limited by dimensions of time and space, there are no limits. This indeed is what the poem says. The poem begins:

> Had we but World enough, and Time, . . .

'Supposing we were freed from the laws of time and space. . . .' It is 'supposing' for, of course, Marvell knows very well – only too well – that he and his mistress are not free. Starting with the Conditional 'Had we' (and we notice that by the simple exchange of the natural-sounding order – 'we had' – for one requiring a strong emphasis on the first element, a final difference is effected between a statement of a past *fact* and a desired situation which can *never* be arrived at), there is an extended disporting in the Subjunctive – the impossible possible. Yet Marvell is not doing as Romantic poets, lovers and lunatics do: deluding himself that subjunctive *is* indicative. Remembering the stress on his first word, Marvell is playing a game, and knows that he is playing a game. He knows, and we know, that this play at 'choosing within the subjunctive' is to be *set against* a knowledge of unalterable indicatives, even though a statement of that knowledge is to be deliberately withheld until the opening of the second paragraph with its famous shock:

> But at my back I alwaies hear
> Times winged Charriot . . .

followed by a series of notes on the checks to will imposed by death and the laws of space. Marvell is not going to assert subjunctive truth as did Shakespeare in his Final Plays; rather he is going to expose the folly of dwelling in hope and the consequent need for immediate action.

But to watch him at his game. Granting the initial premise, then what *would* 'we' do? he asks. Yet it is not quite that, for there is no 'we' – no wit-ness – so long as coyness puts space between them; there is no 'we' until their two strengths and sweetnesses are in 'one Ball'; rather it is a question of what 'I would' and 'you should' do:

> Thou by the *Indian Ganges* side
> Should'st Rubies find: I by the Tide
> Of *Humber* would complain. I would
> Love you ten years before the Flood;
> And you should if you please refuse
> Till the Conversion of the *Jews*.

So it is at the beginning of their pretended enfranchisement from the laws of time and space. But the pretended situation develops. He has a lover's duties ('should's' or 'ought's') as well as a lover's desires ('would's'), and he ought to pay the tribute, in measure of time, that her beauty deserves:

> An hundred years should go to praise
> Thine Eyes, and on thy Forehead Gaze.
> Two hundred to adore each Breast:
> But thirty thousand to the rest.

(Here, it will be noticed, that as his gaze travels down her naked length, the tribute owed to her parts, and expressed by measures of time, naturally increases!)

Thus, supposing what is impossible to be possible, Marvell plays within the one Mood that does allow freedom of play. The lover has a persistency of desire (he 'would') where the will is free; his mistress has persistency of choice (she 'should – if she pleases'). It might seem that the paragraph is a product of fancy which, as Coleridge tells us:

> . . . is indeed no other than a mode of memory emancipated from the order of time and space; while it is blended with, and modified by that empirical phenomenon of the will, which we express by the word Choice.[1]

But I do not here imply – though Coleridge does – any inferiority of fancy with respect to any other power. The fancy of the first paragraph of *To his Coy Mistress* is necessary to the structure of argument of the whole poem.

Desiring and choosing are both subjunctive activities and, being independent of the indicative laws of space, partake of heaven – with this difference: in heaven (who knows!) the desiring and choosing of one solitary will attains satisfaction, and so end; but, on earth, two wills are necessary; two choices must coincide: the lover's *and* his mistress's. Here, on earth, within the freedom of the subjunctive, he is prepared to await, for as long as *she* chooses, the time (desire demanding satisfaction, even the Subjunctive has its, albeit ghostly, Future) when he and she will be in 'one Ball'. But:

> . . . at my back I alwaies hear
> Times winged Charriot hurrying near:
> And yonder all before us lye
> Desarts of vast *Eternity*.

Though in the first paragraph Marvell had played the fancy of pretended freedom from the laws of time and space, *supposing* himself and his mistress to have an eternity in which to dally, yet he reminds her and us that they will have 'desarts' of that soon. That 'vast Eternity' is an indicative certainty and the second paragraph is one of indicative reminders. Indicatively we are bound by time and space for a few years. After that death. And, whatever death is, it will certainly not bring one thing: the opportunity for their bodies to get into 'one Ball'. But that opportunity certainly exists *now* – in the Indicative. It will, with equal certainty, not exist – even the most orthodox will be constrained to admit this – in the 'Desarts of vast Eternity', or at most – if we can allow the indicative and temporal into the context – not until the Resurrection, and then dubitably. And, even if indubitably, then differently because the bodies will be of a different kind.

Thus, placed in the Indicative, the second paragraph is properly a catalogue of reminders of the conditions on the recognition of which the conjugation of the Indicative Mood is precisely constructed. The conditions are of time and space:

> Thy Beauty shall no more be found;
> Nor, in thy marble Vault, shall sound
> My ecchoing Song: then Worms shall try . . .

The insistency of the auxiliary 'shall' tells us that though the whole of the second paragraph is cast into one Mood – *contra* that Mood of the first paragraph – yet the focus is, in fact, narrower still than that. Except for the generally true statements of its last two lines, it is cast into a single Tense of that Mood – the Future. *Future* facts or certainties are stated. In the context of their paragraph they have their powerful effect, less in themselves than because they occur in a paragraph that is of verbial purity. The facts derive their power from the paragraph and the paragraph derives its power because, engineered all in one Tense and Mood, it follows the first paragraph which is engineered purely in another Mood. Yet is is not so much that the two paragraphs conflict, as that they contrast. For, in seeking *to enjoy* (an activity, demanding a verb) his Mistress Marvell discovers two prospects to her: one pretending to offer gratification in the end – but this is known to be illusory; the other of a state, soon to be reached, where there can be no enjoyment of anything. Each prospect is governed by a Verb Form; the first by a form where Time is evaded, the other by a form where Time determines. One prospect is unreal, the other real and barren. Neither offers a course of action within the terms of the verb *to enjoy*. This reduces the hope of action to one Tense – the Present.

As the subjunctive 'would's' and 'should's' ruled the first paragraph; and as the auxiliary 'shall', denoting future certainty, ruled the second paragraph; so does the adverb of time 'now' followed by a First Person plural 'let us' (for *to enjoy* love, the choice must be mutual) of the Imperative Mood, rule the last paragraph:

> Now therefore, while the youthful hew
> .   .   .   .
> Now let us sport us while we may:
> And now, like am'rous birds of prey,
> Rather at once our Time devour,
> Than languish in his slow-chapt pow'r.
> Let us roll . . .

In a frame of the Imperative, the Mood not of present enjoyment but of invitation to present enjoyment, the present action unreally exists. Unreally, for if the poet's 'strength' and his mistress's 'sweetness' were actually rolled up 'into one Ball' there would be no need to plead for that state or action. The meaning of the Verb, and not the word for it, would be a present experienced. Nor – then – would any of the poem be necessary. The point of arguing this is that the last two lines of the paragraph (which like its predecessors is in a different tense from the rest of the unit which it concludes) *suggest* that a translation from the Imperative to the Present Indicative had been made. In fact, of course, the poet is anticipating.

We have said enough, I think, to show that the structure of *To his Coy Mistress* is rigorously determined by its Verb Forms. It is a poem in three sections in three contrasting Tenses and Moods, each section, having adopted its chosen Tense or Mood, remaining pure in its choice. It is this dominance of the Verbs, and Marvell's respect of the laws of time and space – the Personal Pronouns being at the mercy of the nouns of which they are the subject or complement – and with the freedom of choice restricted to freedom within these laws – which this dominance implies, that makes the poem so severely classical and gives it that 'tough reasonableness' of which Mr Eliot speaks.[2]

SOURCE: extract from *Poets' Grammar: Person, Time and Mood in Poetry* (London, 1958), pp. 106–10.

NOTES

[Reorganised and renumbered from the original – Ed.]

1. Coleridge, *Biographia Literaria* (1817), ch. XIII.
2. [Ed.] T. S. Eliot, article on Andrew Marvell, *Times Literary Supplement* (31 March 1921); reproduced in *Selected Essays* (London, 1932; 3rd edition, 1951), p. 293.

Bernard Groom 'The Latin Element in Milton's Diction' (1955)

. . . The most conspicuous general feature of Milton's diction is the large Latin element, and for this he is apt to be blamed by certain recent critics. It must be remembered, however, that there was a difference between the practice of his time and of ours. Many of the words derived from Latin in *Paradise Lost* are simply part of the literary diction of the sixteenth and seventeenth centuries; and, indeed, some of those which strike the modern reader may be found lingering into the age of Victoria. Various words supposed to be examples of Milton's tendency to 'Latinism' will in fact be found in the writings of Spenser, Sylvester, Donne, Dryden, Wordsworth, Shelley, Tennyson, and even Dickens. Nor was Milton by any means alone in coining words from Latin for his own use: even so domestic a writer as Herrick . . . frequently did the same thing. It is impossible, without reference to the authorities, to distinguish between the words which Milton coined and those which were in general currency. For example, *effulgence* and *divulg'd* ('made common') were apparently introduced in *Paradise Lost* (III 388; VII 583); but *circumfluous* and *transpicuous* (VII 270; VIII 141), which might seem to be in the same class, were already in use. In the following paragraphs the reader is referred to the end-notes which distinguish between the Latinisms which Milton introduced and those which independently belong to literary English.

Derivatives from Latin are most apt to attract attention when they are used in their literal, rather than in their acquired English, sense. Latinisms of this kind are so frequent in *Paradise Lost* that in any discussion of Milton's diction an ample list of specimens must be given.

Examples are: 'while Night *invests*[1] the sea' (I 207-8); 'There went a *fame*[2] [i.e., rumour] in Heaven' (I 651); 'Let none *admire*[3] [i.e., marvel] that riches grow in Hell' (I

690–1); '[bees] . . . *expatiate*[4] and confer Thir State affairs' (I 774–5); 'by *success*[5] [i.e., the issue] untaught' (II 9); 'his look *denounc'd*[6] [i.e., proclaimed] Desperate revenge' (II 106–7); 'Will he, so wise, let loose at one his ire, Belike through *impotence*[7] [i.e., lack of self-restraint]' (II 155–6); 'like a Furnace mouth cast forth *redounding*[8] smoak' (II 888–9); 'the sacred *influence*[9] Of light' (II 1034–5); 'His habit fit for speed *succinct*[10] . . .' (III 643); 'mazie *error*[11] [i.e., wandering] under pendent shades' (IV 239); 'Or if, *inspiring*[12] venom, he might taint Th'animal Spirits that from pure blood arise' (IV 804–5); 'warne him to beware He swerve not too *secure*[13] [i.e., confident]' (V 237–8); 'in fight they stood Unwearied, *unobnoxious*[14] to be pain'd' (VI 403–4); 'Night her course began . . . *Inducing*[15] darkness' (VI 406–7); 'Heav'n *ruining*[16] [i.e., falling headlong] from Heav'n' (VI 868); (of rivers) 'with *Serpent*[17] errour wandring' (VII 302); 'Bush with frizl'd hair *implicit*[18] . . .' (VII 323); 'some of the Serpent kinde . . . *involv'd*[19] Thir Snakie foulds' (VII 482–4); 'his circling Spires, that on the grass Floted *redundant*[20] . . .' (IX 502–3); '*pontifical*[21] [i.e., bridgemaking]' (X 313); 'A monstrous Serpent on his Belly prone, *Reluctant*[22] [i.e., writhing]' (X 514–15); 'Who can *extenuate*[23] [i.e., diminish] thee?' (X 645); 'by envious windes Blow'n *vagabond*[24] . . .' (XI 15–16); 'his taste of that *defended*[25] [i.e., forbidden] Fruit' (XI 85–6); 'to the evil turne My *obvious*[26] breast' (XI 373–4); 'what thou livst Live well, how long or short *permit*[27] to Heav'n' (XI 549–50); 'Led them direct, and down the Cliff as fast To the *subjected*[28] plaine' (XII 639–40).

Secondly, there are the Latin derivaties which attract attention by some unusual feature in their form; for instance, the passive participial forms without English inflexion.

Examples are: 'thoughts more *elevate*[29] . . .' (II 558); 'Bright effluence of bright essence *increate*[30] [i.e., uncreated]' (III 6); 'the main Abyss Wide *interrupt*[31] . . .' (III 83–4); 'with *submiss*[32] approach' (V 359); '*alienate*[33] from God' (V 877).

Some of the present participles from Latin have a distinctly foreign air. For example: '*nocent*[34] . . .' (IX 186); '*Ponent*[35] Windes' (X 704); '*plenipotent*[36] . . .' (X 404); '*fulgent*[37] . . .' (X 449); '*peccant*[38] . . .' (XI 70); 'his *volant*[39] touch' (XI 561).

Among the rarer words of Latin origin are: '*opacous*' (III 418); '*magnific* Titles' (V 773); 'warr in *procinct*[40] . . .' (VI 19: Latin 'in procinctu'); '*petrific*[41] . . .' (X 294); '*appetence*[42] . . .' (XI 619).

Lastly, certain of Milton's English words are suggestive of Latin usage rather than native idiom. *Shade* for 'umbra' and *grove* for 'nemus' are common. Other instances are: the use of *strive* for 'certare' – 'nor that sweet Grove . . . might with this Paradise of Eden *strive*[43] . . .' (IV 275) – and of *kind* for 'genus', as in 'the total *kind* of Birds' (VI 73–4).

Milton's Latinism is in some measure his deliberate choice, and it is natural to ask what reasons there are for this pronounced feature of his style. The question cannot be answered simply, for the reasons are numerous and complex. One motive is variety. Milton's theme is a vast one, but without the help of art it would be dangerously void. The use of elaborate language helps to fill the vacuity and to disguise the uniformity. Many things in his unfilled Universe have to be mentioned more than once, and Latinisms, like periphrases,[44] may conceal the repetition.

The central act of *Paradise Lost*, on which such enormous issues depend, is the eating of an apple. Even in an age of Bible-worship, the use of a word so simple as *apple* in a style so magnificent as Milton's was dangerous. Satan scornfully mentions 'the apple' by name when he is boasting in Hell of his success (X 487); but in Milton's lofty invocation it is called 'the fruit of that forbidden tree' (I 1–2). It cannot be so named again, and when there is need for another periphrasis, Milton takes refuge in a Latinism and calls it 'that *defended* Fruit' (XI 86).

A second motive is the desire to give reality to actions and scenes outside experience, and almost beyond imagination. Milton's memory for the historical and fabulous analogies which bear on the course of his narrative is the chief solution for this difficulty, but he is also helped by his profound knowledge of words. A technical term may sometimes seem to lend the sanction of science to a fiction of poetry.

An example is the word *influence*: an astrological word for the effect of stars or planets on human destiny. It was not so rare as

to seem pedantic, and it is a word with a solid core of thought.
Milton uses it with fine effect at the end of Book II. Satan,
having escaped from Hell, has just passed through the wild
confusion and 'eternal anarchy' of Chaos, and looks up at last
to the world of unalterable law:

> But now at last the *sacred influence*
> Of light appears, and from the walls of Heav'n
> Shoots farr into the bosom of dim Night
> A glimmering dawn.   (II 1034–7)

A third motive for Latinisms was to create contrast. Milton's
vast learning left intact his poetic love of native words, and no
one has felt more keenly the beauty of biblical English. Such
language loses its force by repetition or over-use; it must be
blended with exotic words, or reserved for crucial moments.

A striking instance of its effect, heightened by contrast
occurs in Book IX. Milton has first to describe the beauty of the
serpent before the Fall, and as this is invention he weaves an
elaborate tissue of artificial words:

> him fast sleeping soon he [Satan] found
> In Labyrinth of many a round self-rowld,
> His head the midst, well stor'd with suttle wiles:
> Not yet in horrid Shade or dismal Den,
> Not nocent yet, but on the grassie Herbe
> Fearless unfeard he slept.   (IX 182–7)

In the awful moment of the Temptation (Book IX), Milton
keeps close to the biblical account, altering its words only with
the slightest touches for the sake of metre; but he inserts one
phrase of his own, introducing Eve's answer to the tempter
with the words:

> To whom thus Eve *yet sinless* . . .   (IX 659)

The difference in effect between words like *nocent* (or *peccant*)
and *sinless* suggests one main principle of Milton's diction.
Latinisms are employed to give his style 'material sublimity':
they create grandeur of sound and splendour of allusion; they
are a 'glistering foil'. But for 'moral sublimity', he depends on
simpler means. Neither kind of diction would produce its full
effect by itself; but, used in appropriate places, each enhances

and enforces the other. The three main uses of Milton's Latinisms, then, are for variety, solidity, and contrast. . . .

SOURCE: extract from *The Diction of Poetry from Spenser to Bridges* (Toronto, 1955), pp. 81–5.

NOTES

[Reorganised and renumbered from the original – Ed.]

1. *Invests* = covers: the original sense in literary English.

2. *Fame* = rumour: 'now rare' (*OED*), but an established literary usage in Milton's time.

3. *Admire* = marvel: archaic now, but found even as late as Dickens.

4. *Expatiate* = wander around: 'now somewhat rare in the literal sense' (*OED*).

5. *Success* = issue, outcome, obsolete, but found with this usage between 1537 and 1733.

6. *Denounc'd* = proclaimed: 'obsolete' (*OED*, which cites Johnson's *Rambler* for its last example).

7. *Impotence* = lack of self-restraint: a common seventeenth-century sense, but the usual form is 'impotency'.

8. *Redounding* = overflowing: also used in this sense by Spenser.

9. *Influence*: established in this astrological sense in literary English since the time of Chaucer.

10. *Succinct* = girded: 'archaic or poetic' (*OED*, which gives this instance as its first example).

11. *Error* = wandering: 'now only poetic – in French and English it occurs only as a conscious imitation of Latin usage' (*OED*).

12. *Inspiring* = breathing upon or into: also in Spenser and Dryden.

13. *Secure* = confident: formerly common in literary English.

14. *Unobnoxious* = not liable: also in Donne and Wordsworth.

15. *Inducing* = leading on, bringing in: a little unusual with such a word as 'darkness'.

16. *Ruining* = falling headlong: found before Milton; also in Shelley, Tennyson etc.

17. *Serpent* = serpentine, sinuous: so used by Sylvester.

18. *Implicit* = entwined, entangled: 'obsolete' (*OED*); the sense here is unusual, though not confined to Milton.

19. *Involv'd* = enfolded, twined: unusual, but an author in 1555 writes, 'involved after the manner of a sleeping snake'.

20. *Redundant* = overflowing, wave-like: 'obsolete' (*OED*, which cites this as its first example, giving only one other – from Pope's *Odyssey*).

21. *Pontifical* = bridge-making: this is the first example given by the *OED* of the word as used in this 'reputed etymological sense'.

22. *Reluctant* = writhing: 'rare' (*OED*, which cites this as its first example, giving only one other – from Shelley).

23. *Extenuate* = diminish: this sense 'obsolete' (*OED*).

24. *Vagabond* = hither-and-thither: cited in *OED* as a figurative use of the word.

25. *Defended* = forbidden: 'obsolete' (*OED*, which cites Milton's use as its last example); 'fruyt defendid' is in Chaucer.

26. *Obvious* = outward turning, confronting: 'obsolete or archaic' (*OED*, which cites examples from literary use between 1603 and 1814).

27. *Permit* = leave to, entrust: 'obsolete' (*OED*).

28. *Subjected* = lying below: 'obsolete or archaic' (*OED*).

29. *Elevate* = lofty: 'from 18th c. only poetic' (*OED*, which cites Chaucer for its earliest example).

30. *Increate* = uncreated: *OED* notes that Lydgate has 'Mighty loue eterne and increat', which is almost Miltonic.

31. *Interrupt* = interrupted, divided: *OED* cites examples from Lydgate and others, with its last example from Milton.

32. *Submiss*: submissive: 'obsolete or archaic' (*OED*, which quotes examples in literary use between 1570 and 1904).

33. *Alienate* = alienated: the earliest *OED* example is from Lydgate, 1430.

34. *Nocent* = harmful: 'now rare' (*OED*).

35. *Ponent* = heavy, strong, 'obsolete or archaic' (*OED*); used in descriptive writing before Milton.

36. *Plenipotent* = all-powerful: 'rare' (*OED*, which dates its first example 1658).

37. *Fulgent* = shining, intensely bright: 'now poetic or rhetorical' (*OED*).

38. *Peccant* = sinning: so used by Giles Fletcher, 1610.

39. *Volant* = fluttering, nimble: Milton's figurative use has been sometimes copied.

40. *Procinct* = preparation: 'obsolete; only in *In procinct*, ready, prepared' (*OED*, which cites its first example from Chapman's *Iliad*).

41. *Petrific* = turning to stone: this is the first example cited in *OED*.

42. *Appetence* = longing for, seeking after: the first example in *OED* is from Giles Fletcher, 1610.

43. *Strive* = rival, vie with: the use of *strive* in this sense is found in Chaucer, and even earlier; but I find it hard not to believe that in Milton the word is based on the Latin idiom.

44. [Ed.] Periphrasis: lit. 'walking about'; in the lexis of literary style it may mean 'circumlocution' or (as here) alternative expressions for the same thing, the use of synonyms.

Christopher Ricks 'Syntax and Sublimity in *Paradise Lost*' (1963)

. . . there are times when Milton deviates from the usual word-order for the bad reason that he is in the habit of it. And there are times when he does so for the inadequate and well-known reason that the result sounds more magniloquent, or – in Addison's phrase – 'to give his Verse the greater Sound, and throw it out of Prose'. Yet it is interesting that Addison went on to say, 'I must confess, that I think his Stile, tho' admirable in general, is in some Places too much stiffened and obscured by the frequent Use of those Methods, which *Aristotle* has prescribed for the raising of it'. [See excerpt in Part One, above – Ed.] But this, as he saw, does not apply to the usual run of the verse, in which the syntax is meaningfully controlled with great success.

Its first success is obvious enough: his natural port was gigantic loftiness. Milton achieves this loftiness as much by word-order as by the sonority, dignity or weight of the words themselves. Mr Eliot has put the positive side excellently:

. . . It is only in the period that the wave-length of Milton's verse is to be found: it is his ability to give a perfect and unique pattern to every paragraph, such that the full beauty of the line is found in its context, and his ability to work in larger musical units than any other poet – that is to me the most conclusive evidence of Milton's supreme mastery. The peculiar feeling, almost a physical sensation of a breathless leap, communicated by Milton's long periods, and by his alone, is impossible to procure from rhymed verse. . . .[1]

The power and sublimity of a 'breathless leap' are there in the opening lines of the poem:

Of Mans First Disobedience, and the Fruit
Of that Forbidden Tree, whose mortal tast
Brought Death into the World, and all our woe,
With loss of Eden, till one greater Man
Restore us, and regain the blissful Seat,
Sing Heav'nly Muse, . . .

Matthew Arnold acutely commented: 'So chary of a sentence is he, so resolute not to let it escape him till he has crowded into it all he can, that it is not till the thirty-ninth word in the sentence that he will give us the key to it, the word of action, the verb.'[2]

But such withholding of the verb 'sing' (*Of Mans First Disobedience . . . Sing*) might be no more than perverse. Its justification is in the heroic way that it states the magnitude of the poem's subject and so the magnitude of its task

    (*Disobedience . . . Death . . . woe . . . loss of Eden . . . one greater Man*),

while still insisting that this vastness is within the poet's compass. The word-order quite literally encompasses the huge themes. 'Where couldst thou words of such a compass find?' asked Marvell, wondering at Milton's achievement of his *vast Design*: 'a Work so infinite he spann'd'.

A poet is always insisting, as if by magic, that his control of words is a control of experience; and here we are given a 'breathless' sense of Milton's *adventrous Song* with at the same time a reassuring sense of how firmly it is within his control. The curve of the sentence is not discursive – however wide the gyre, this falcon hears its falconer.

The verb is, as Arnold saw, the 'key' to the sentence – in the sense that it embodies Milton's power to open the subjects of his poem. Yet we would not be very interested in, or impressed by, a key unless we had first been given some idea of what riches we will be shown.

'So *resolute* not to let it escape him . . .', said Arnold, and the word may be used as a transition to a fine comment by Mr Empson. He quotes Valdes's lines to Faustus, lines which deliberately hold back until the end the ominous condition *If learned Faustus will be resolute*:

                Faustus,
These books, thy wit, and our experience,
Shall make all nations to canonise us.
As Indian moors obey their Spanish lords
So shall the spirits of every element
Be always serviceable to us three;
Like lions shall they guard us when we please,

> Like Almain rutters, with their horsemen's staves,
> Or Lapland giants, trotting by our sides,
> Sometimes like women, or unwedded maids
> Shadowing more beauty in their airy brows
> Than have the white breasts of the queen of love:
> From Venice shall they drag huge argosies,
> And from America the golden fleece
> That yearly stuffs old Philip's treasury;
> If learned Faustus will be resolute.

'That a conditional clause should have been held back through all these successive lightnings of poetry, that after their achievement it should still be present with the same conviction and *resolution*, is itself a statement of heroic character.'[3] That is nobly said, and such heroism is one of Milton's glories too. He is even able to sustain such effects over vaster distances. Though his single lines may not be mightier than Marlow's, his sentences often are.

Take Belial's reply to Moloch during the council in Hell. Moloch has asked rhetorically 'what can be worse than to dwell here', and Belial seizes the phrase and holds it aloft:

> What can we suffer worse? is this then worst,
> Thus sitting, thus consulting, thus in Arms?

And at once he launches his argument, wheeling through six lines with a hawk's-eye view of their past torments, and plunging home with *that sure was worse*. But that telling reminder offers no pause, and Belial circles again, this time above their future torments. He drives relentlessly through 'what if . . . or . . . what if . . .', and then sweeps to his annihilating climax, foreseen and deliberately held back:

> What if the breath that kindl'd those grim fires
> Awak'd should blow them into sevenfold rage
> And plunge us in the Flames? or from above
> Should intermitted vengeance Arme again
> His red right hand to plague us? what if all
> Her stores were op'n'd, and this Firmament
> Of Hell should spout her Cataracts of Fire,
> Impendent horrors, threatning hideous fall
> One day upon our heads; while we perhaps
> Designing or exhorting glorious Warr,
> Caught in a fierie Tempest shall be hurl'd

Each on his rock transfixt, the sport and prey
Of racking whirlwinds, or for ever sunk
Under yon boyling Ocean, wrapt in Chains;
There to converse with everlasting groans,
Unrespited, unpitied, unrepreevd,
Ages of hopeless end; this would be worse.   [II 170–86]

When a sentence surges forward like that, the end of it seems
less a destination than a destiny.

It is this ability to harness the thrust of his syntax which
sustains Milton's great argument – even the smallest passages
have a dynamic force of the astonishing kind which one finds
almost everywhere in Dickens. And lines which one has long
admired for their brilliant succinctness, lines like 'Better to
reign in Hell, then serve in Heav'n' which from one point of
view have the free-standing strength of proverbs – even such
lines take on greater force when they come as the clinching of a
surge of feeling:

What matter where, if I be still the same,
And what I should be, all but less then hee
Whom Thunder hath made greater? Here at least
We shall be free; th' Almighty hath not built
Here for his envy, will not drive us hence:
Here we may reign secure, and in my choyce
To reign is worth ambition though in Hell:
Better to reign in Hell, then serve in Heav'n.   [I 256–63]

It is easy to see how much the power of the last line is created
by its context if we remember Dryden's setting in *The State of
Innocence*. In Dryden the line is witty:

Chang'd as we are, we'er yet from Homage free;
We have, by Hell, at least, gain'd liberty:
That's worth our fall; thus low tho' we are driven,
Better to Rule in Hell, than serve in Heaven.   [Act I]

Yet in Milton the line was not the less witty for being
heroic. . . .

SOURCE: extract from *Milton's Grand Style* (Oxford, 1963),
pp. 27–31.

NOTES

[Reorganised from the original – Ed.]

1. T. S. Eliot, essay on Milton, first published in 1947; reproduced as 'Milton II' in *On Poetry and Poets* (London, 1957), pp. 157–8.
2. Matthew Arnold, *On Translating Homer*, III (1861).
3. William Empson, *Seven Types of Ambiguity* (Cambridge, 1930; 2nd edition, 1947), p. 32.

Geoffrey Tillotson 'Onomatopoeia in Pope and Tennyson' (1938)

. . . Onomatopoeia is a childish effect if it is carried to the extent to which, for instance, Tennyson carried it in the *Idylls*. So ding'd with consonants is a tournament in the *Idylls* that the sounds predominate over the sense. They invite a standard of judgement which is not literary but sonoral. One is made to test the words as an adjudicator at a musical festival would test sound. In his tournaments Tennyson seems to be expecting to produce the actual sounds, rather than to suggest them. The result is that instead of an effect of the deafening clash of real armour against armour, he provides a tintinnabulation which reminds one of the clockwork tournament in Wells Cathedral.

If one neglects Pope's Homer, it would be fair to both Pope and Tennyson to place Tennyson's

The moan of doves in immemorial elms

beside Pope's

With all the mournful family of Yews.   [*Moral Essays*, IV 96]

In the first place Tennyson is characteristically trying to produce actual sounds, whereas Pope is translating into mournful sound a mournful visual effect. Moreover, in Pope the line, though serious in itself, is intended in its context to have a comic effect. Pope is amused at the changing fashions in gardens:

> Thro' his young Woods how pleas'd Sabinus stray'd,
> Or sat delighted in the thick'ning shade,
> With annual joy the redd'ning shoots to greet,
> Or see the stretching branches long to meet!
> His Son's fine Taste an op'ner Vista loves,
> Foe to the Dryads of his Father's groves;
> One boundless Green, or flourish'd Carpet views,
> With all the mournful family of Yews;
> The thriving plants ignoble broomsticks made,
> Now sweep those Alleys they were born to shade.

The content of Pope's line is more satisfactory than that of Tennyson's; more valuable as poetry than *immemorial elms*. The image of a dove in an elm tree is not so good as the line is musical. Elm trees are whiskery and coarse trees unless seen at a distance, and at a distance the moan of their doves would be inaudible. This happens with the line, if one neglects the music. In practice one cannot neglect the music. It is much too potent. But the result is that the elm trees are not real ones. The line makes one suspend the working of the brain and accept sounds instead. This is a too ready magic, for a great poet. Pope does not allow music to smother sense and his line is the finer because of it. *Mournful family of yews* brings out qualities that are actually there in yews. Pope writes, as Wordsworth counselled, with his eye on the object, and so his ear is kept in its right place, of its right size. Tennyson shuts his eye and extends an ear like a gramophone horn. He shows himself as a Liszt *manqué*, not as an artist in words. . . .

SOURCE: extract from *On the Poetry of Pope* (Oxford, 1938; 2nd edition, 1950), pp. 119–21.

William Empson   'Ambiguity in Keats's *Ode on Melancholy*'   (1930)

. . . Keats often used ambiguities of this type to convey a dissolution of normal experience into intensity of sensation. This need not be concentrated into an ambiguity.

> Let the rich wine within the goblet boil
>   Cold as a bubbling well

is an example of what I mean; and the contrast between cold weather and the heat of passion which is never forgotten throughout *St Agnes' Eve*. It is the 'going hot and cold at once' of fever. The same method is worth observing in detail when in the *Ode [on] Melancholy* it pounds together the sensations of joy and sorrow till they combine into sexuality.

> No, no: go not to Lethe, neither twist
>   Wolf's-bane, tight-rooted, for its poisonous wine:
> Nor suffer thy pale forehead to be kissed
>   By nightshade, ruby grape of Proserpine;
> Make not your rosary of yewberries,
>   Nor let the beetle nor the death-moth be
>   Your mournful Psyche, nor the downy owl
> A partner in your sorrow's mysteries;
>   For shade to shade will come too drowsily,
>   And dull the wakeful anguish of the soul.

One must enjoy the didactic tone of this great anthology piece; it is a parody, by contradiction, of the wise advice of uncles. 'Of course, pain is what we all desire, and I am sure I hope you will be very unhappy. But if you go snatching at it before your time, my boy, you must expect the consequences; you will hardly get hurt at all.'

'Do not abandon yourself to melancholy, delightful as that would be, or you will lose the sensations of incipient melancholia. Do not think always about forgetting, or you will forget its pain. Do not achieve death, or you can no longer live in its shadow. Taste rather at their most sharp the full sensations of death, of melancholy, and of oblivion.' But I have paraphrased only for my own pleasure; there is no need for me to insist on the contrariety of the pathological splendours of this introduction.

Opposite notions combined in this poem include death and the sexual act, a pair of which I must produce further examples; pain and pleasure, perhaps as a milder version of this; the conception of the woman as at once mistress and mother, at once soothing and exciting, whom one must master, to whom one must yield; a desire at once for the eternity of fame and for the irresponsibility of oblivion; an apprehension of ideal beauty as sensual; and an apprehension of eternal beauty as fleeting. The perfection of form, the immediacy of statement, of the Ode, lie in the fact that these are all collected into the single antithesis which unites Melancholy to Joy. Biographers who attempt to show from Keats's life how he came by these notions are excellently employed, but it is no use calling them in to explain why the poem is so universally intelligible and admired; evidently these pairs of opposites, stated in the right way, make a direct appeal to the normal habits of the mind.

> But when the melancholy fit shall fall
>   Sudden from Heaven like a weeping cloud,
> That fosters the droop-headed flowers all,
>   And hides the green hill in an April shroud;

Weeping produces the flowers of joy which are themselves sorrowful; the *hill* is *green* as young, fresh and springing, or with age, mould and geology; *April* is both rainy and part of springtime; and the *shroud*, an anticipation of death that has its own energy and beauty, either is itself the fact that the old *hill* is hidden under *green*, or is itself the grey mist, the greyness of falling rain, which is reviving that verdure.

> Then glut thy sorrow on a morning rose,
>   Or on the rainbow of the salt sand wave,
>   Or on the wealth of globed peonies.

Either: 'Give rein to sorrow, at the mortality of beauty', or 'defeat sorrow by sudden excess and turn it to joy, at the intensity of sensation'. *Morning* is parallel to *April*, and pun with mourning; the flowers stand at once for the more available forms of beauty, and for the *mistress* who is unkind.

> Or if thy mistress some rich anger shows
>> Imprison her soft hand, and let her rave,
>>> And feed deep, deep upon her peerless eyes.
>
> She dwells with Beauty, Beauty that must die,
>> And Joy, whose hand is ever at his lips,
> Bidding adieu, and aching Pleasure nigh,
>> Turning to poison while the bee-mouth sips;
> Aye, in the very Temple of Delight
>> Veiled Melancholy hath her sovran shrine.

She is at first *thy mistress*, so that she represents some degree of *joy*, however fleeting; then, taking the verse as a unit, she becomes *Veiled Melancholy* itself; *veiled* like a widow or holding up a handkerchief for sorrow, or *veiled*, like the hill under its *green*, because at first sight *joy*. *Very* and *sovran*, with an air of making a distinction and overcoming the casual prejudice of the reader, now insist that this new sort of *joy* is in part a fusion of *joy* and *melancholy*; *sovran* means either 'melancholy is here deepest,' or 'this new production is the satisfactory (and attractive) kind of melancholy'; and she is *veiled* because only in the mystery of her ambivalence is true *joy* to be found.

> Though seen of none save him whose strenuous tongue
>> Can burst joy's grape against his palate fine;

'Can burst the distinction between the two opposites; can discover the proud and sated melancholy to which only those are entitled who have completed an activity and achieved joy.'

> His soul shall taste the sadness of her might
>> And be among her cloudy trophies hung.

If *sadness* here was taken as an attribute of *melancholy* only, as the only unambiguous reading must insist, we should have a tautology which no amount of historical allusion could make sensible; though *melancholy* meant Burton and Hamlet and *sadness* meant seriousness, it would still be like Coleridge's parody:

> So sad and miff; oh I feel *very* sad.

She has become *joy*, *melancholy*, and the beautiful but occasionally raving *mistress*; the grandeur of the line is unquestioned only because everybody takes this for granted.

Her trophies (death-pale are they all) are *cloudy* because vague and faint with the intensity and puzzling character of this fusion, or because already dead, or because, though preserved in verse, irrevocable. They are *hung* because sailors on escaping shipwreck hung up votive gifts in gratitude [Horace, III i], or because, so far from having escaped, in the swoon of this achievement he has lost life, independence, and even distinction from her.

No doubt most people would admit that this is how Keats gets his effects, but the words are not obviously ambiguous because, in the general wealth of the writing, it is possible to spread out one to each word the meanings which are actually diffused into all of them. . . .

SOURCE: extract from *Seven Types of Ambiguity* (London, 1930; 3rd edition, 1963), pp. 214–17.

F. R. Leavis   'Keats's *Ode to a Nightingale*' (1936)

. . . The Ode, it has been said above, tends to suffer an unfair simplification in memory; the thought of its being 'rich to die,' and the desire

> To cease upon the midnight with no pain,

tend to stand for more of it than they should. Actually, when we re-read it we find that it moves outwards and upwards towards life as strongly as it moves downwards towards extinction; the Ode is, in fact, an extremely subtle and varied interplay of motions, directed now positively, now negatively. Consider the opening stanza:

> My heart aches, and a drowsy numbness pains
> My sense, as though of hemlock I had drunk,
> Or emptied some dull opiate to the drains
> One minute past, and Lethe-wards had sunk:
> 'Tis not through envy of thy happy lot,
> But being too happy in thine happiness, –
> That thou, light-wingèd Dryad of the trees,
> In some melodious plot
> Of beechen green, and shadows numberless,
> Singest of summer in full-throated case.

It starts Lethe-wards, with a heavy drugged movement ('drowsy', 'numb', 'dull') down to 'sunk'. The part played by the first line-division is worth noting – the difference the division makes to the phrase 'a drowsy numbness pains my sense'. In the fifth and sixth lines, with the reiterated 'happy', the direction changes, and in the next line comes the key-word, 'light-wingèd'. The stanza now moves buoyantly towards life, the fresh air and the sunlight ('shadows numberless') – the thought of happy, self-sufficient vitality provides the impulse. The common medium, so to speak, in which the shift of direction takes place with such unobtrusive effectiveness, the pervasive sense of luxury, is given explicitly in the closing phrase of the stanza, 'full-throated ease'.

Down the throat (now the poet's) flows, in the next stanza, the 'draught of vintage',

> Cool'd a long age in the deep-delved earth,

the coolness (having banished the drowsy fever) playing voluptuously against the warmth of 'the warm South'. The sensuous luxury keeps its element of the 'light-wingèd': there are the 'beaded bubbles winking at the brim'. This second stanza reverses the movement of the first; until the last two lines it moves towards life and the stirring human world,

> Dance and Provençal song and sunburnt mirth.

But the optative 'O' changes direction, as if with the changing effect (now no longer excitation) of the wine, and the stanza ends on the desire to

> leave the world unseen
> And with thee fade away into the forest dim.

The next stanza is the only one in the poem to be completely disintoxicated and disenchanted. It is notable how at the second line the tone, the manner of reading compelled on one, alters, turning from incantatory into prosaic matter-of-fact:

> Fade far away, dissolve, and quite forget
>   What thou among the leaves hast never known,
> The weariness, the fever, and the fret
>   Here, where men sit and hear each other groan;
> Where palsy shakes a few, sad, last gray hairs,
>   Where youth grows pale, and spectre-thin, and dies . . .

That 'spectre-thin' is a key-word, suggesting as it does, along with 'gray', the thin unreality of the disintoxicated, unbeglamoured moments that the addict dreads.

The fourth stanza takes up the 'away' again – but not the 'fade':

> Away! away! for I will fly to thee,
>   Not charioted by Bacchus and his pards,
> But on the viewless wings of Poesy . . .

It points now, not to dissolution and unconsciousness but to positive satisfactions, concretely realised in imagination: they represent the world of 'Poesy' (for poetry was Poesy to the Keats of *Endymion* and the Odes). We have now the rich evocation of enchantment and delighted senses, and here again the touch of the consummate artist manifests itself; in the very piling up of luxuries a sure delicacy presides:

> I cannot see what flowers are at my feet,
>   Nor what soft incense hangs upon the boughs,
> But, in embalmed darkess, guess each sweet
>   Wherewith the seasonable month endows
> The grass, the thicket and the fruit-tree wild;
>   White hawthorn, and the pastoral eglantine . . .

– the 'grass', the 'thicket' and the cool reminders of the English spring bring the needed note of freshness into the else too cloying accumulation of sweets.

And now comes a stanza that, in the simplifying memory, tends to get undue prominence:

Darkling I listen; and for many a time
  I have been half in love with easeful Death,
Call'd him soft names in many a mused rhyme,
  To take into the air my quiet breath;
Now more than ever seems it rich to die,
To cease upon the midnight with no pain,
  While thou art pouring forth thy soul abroad
    In such an ecstasy!
Still wouldst thou sing, and I have ears in vain –
  To thy high requiem become a sod.

In the re-reading the force of that 'half' comes home to us: Keats is strictly only half in love with death, and the positive motion is present even in this stanza. It is present in the 'rich' of 'rich to die,' a phrase that epitomises the poem. The desire not to die appears in the thought of becoming a sod to the nightingale's high requiem and of having ears in vain, and it swells into a strong revulsion against death in the opening lines of the next stanza:

Thou wast not born for death, immortal Bird!
  No hungry generations tread thee down . . .

Bridges, as a conscientious critic, solemnly points out the fallacy here: 'the thought is fanciful or superficial – the man being as immortal as the bird,' etc. That the thought is fallacious witnesses, of course, to the intensity of the wish that fathered it. Keats entertains at one and the same time the desire to escape into easeful death from 'the weariness, the fever and the fret' –

To cease upon the midnight with no pain,

and the complementary desire for a full life unattended by these disadvantages. And the inappropriateness of the nightingale's song as a symbol of enduring satisfaction –

The voice I hear this passing night was heard
  In ancient days by emperor and clown:
Perhaps the self-same song that found a path
  Through the sad heart of Ruth, when, sick for home,
    She stood in tears amid the alien corn;

– manifests locally the complexity of the impulsions behind the poem. The regressive desire to 'cease upon the midnight' slips, it will be noticed, into the positive nostalgia represented by Ruth, the association of the two providing an interesting illustration to D. W. Harding's *Note on Nostalgia*.[1]

Bridges has also a criticism to make against the opening of the final stanza: the 'introduction', he says, is 'artificial', by which he would seem to suggest that Keats, having earlier in the Ode got his transition, managed his development, by picking up a word or a phrase already used, now mechanically repeats the closing 'forlorn' of the penultimate stanza because he can think of no better way of carrying on:

> The same that oft-times hath
> Charm'd magic casements, opening on the foam
> Of perilous seas, in faery lands forlorn.
>
> Forlorn! the very word is like a bell
> To toll me back from thee to my sole self!
> Adieu! the fancy cannot cheat so well
> As she is fam'd to do, deceiving elf.

Actually, that the repetition has a peculiar and appropriate force is obvious, or would be if Keats had not here suffered the injury incidental to becoming 'hackneyed.' In 'faery lands forlorn' – the adjective has acquired the wrong kind of inevitability; it would but for the hackneying, but for the groove in one's mind, be seen to be, coming with the final emphasis at the end of those two glamorous lines, unexpected. It is so for Keats; he turns it over, and it becomes as he looks at it the recognition upon which the poem ends – the recognition that we, looking back, can see to have been approaching in the passage about Ruth, 'sick for home', which gives us the sickness to contemplate, not the home: even the illusion of a 'secure happiness' as something to be ecstatically, if enviously, contemplated in the nightingale is recognised to be an evanescent indulgence, belonging to the world of 'magic casements, opening on the foam of perilous seas'. The song that fades away is no longer an ecstasy, but a 'plaintive anthem'. . . .

SOURCE: extract from *Revaluation: Tradition and Development in English Poetry* (London, 1936), pp. 245–51.

NOTE

[Reorganised from the original – Ed.]

1. In F. R. Leavis (ed.), *Determinations: Critical Essays* (London, 1934); see especially p. 68.

Randall Jarrell   'A Poem by
A. E. Housman'   (1939)

> Crossing alone the nighted ferry
> With the one coin for fee,
> Whom, on the wharf of Lethe waiting,
> Count you to find? Not me.
>
> The brisk fond lackey to fetch and carry,
> The true, sick-hearted slave,
> Expect him not in the just city
> And free land of the grave.

The first stanza is oddly constructed; it manages to carry over several more or less unexpressed statements, while the statement it makes on the surface, grammatically, is arranged so as to make the reader disregard it completely. Literally, the stanza says *Whom do you expect to find waiting for you? Not me.* But the denying and elliptical *not me* is not an answer to the surface question; that question is almost rhetorical, and obviously gets a *me*; the *not me* denies *And I'll satisfy your expectations and be there?* – the implied corollary of the surface question; and the flippant and brutal finality of the *not me* implies that the expectations are foolish. (A belief that can be contradicted so carelessly and completely – by a person in a position to know – is a foolish one.) The stanza says: *You do expect to find me and ought not to* and

You're actually such a fool as to count on my being there? and *So I'll be there, eh? Not me.*

Some paraphrases of the two stanzas will show how extraordinarily much they do mean; they illustrate the quality of poetry that is almost its most characteristic, compression. These paraphrases are not very imaginative – the reader can find justification for any statement in the actual words of the poem. (Though not in any part considered in isolation. The part as part has a misleading look of independence and reality, just as does the word as word; but it has only that relationship to the larger contexts of the poem that the words which compose it have to it, and its significance is similarly controlled and extended by those larger units of which it is a part. A poem is a sort of onion of contexts, and you can no more locate any of the important meanings exclusively in a part than you can locate a relation in one of its terms. The significance of a part may be greatly modified or even in extreme cases completely reversed by later and larger parts and by the whole. This will be illustrated in the following discussion: most of the important meanings attached to the first stanza do not exist when the stanza is considered in isolation.) And the paraphrases are not hypertrophied, they do not even begin to be exhaustive.

Stanza 1:   Do you expect me to wait patiently for you there, just as I have done on earth? expect that, in Hell, after death, things will go on for you just as they do here on earth? that there, after crossing and drinking Lethe and oblivion, I'll still be thinking of human you, still be waiting faithfully there on the wharf for you to arrive, with you still my only interest, with me still your absolutely devoted slave, – just as we are here? Do you really? Do you actually suppose that you yourself, then, will be able to expect it? Even when dead, all alone, on that grim ferry, in the middle of the dark forgetful river, all that's left of your human life one coin, you'll be stupid or inflexible or faithful enough to *count* on (you're sure, are you, so sure that not even a doubt enters your mind?) finding me waiting there? How are we to understand an inflexibility that seems almost incredible? Is it because you're pathetically deluded about love's constancy, my great lasting love for you? (This version makes the *you* sympathetic; but it is unlikely, an unstressed possibility, and the others do not.) Or is it that you're so sure of my complete enslavement that you know death itself can't change it? Or are you so peculiarly stupid that you can't even conceive of any essential change away from your past life and knowledge, even after the death that has destroyed them both? Or is it the general inescapable stupidity of mankind, who can conceive of death only in human and vital terms? (Housman's not giving the reasons, when the reasons must be thought about if the poem is to be understood, forces the reader to make them for himself, and to see that there is a wide range that must be considered. This is one of the most important principles of compression in poetry; these implied foundations or justifications for a statement might be called *bases*.) Are you actually such a fool as to believe that? So I'll be there? Not me. You're wrong. There things are really different.

One of the most important elements in the poem is the tone of the *not me*. Its casualness, finality, and matter-of-fact bluntness give it almost the effect of slang. It is the crudest of denials. There is in it a laconic brutality, an imperturbable and almost complacent vigor; it has certainly a sort of contempt. Contempt for what? Contempt at himself for his faithlessness? contempt at himself for his obsessing weakness – for not being faithless now instead of then? Or contempt at her, for being bad enough to keep things as they are, for being stupid enough to imagine that they will be so always? The tone is both threatening and disgusted. It shivers between all these qualities like a just-thrown knife. And to what particular denial does this tone attach? how specific, how general a one? These are changes a reader can easily ring for himself; but I hope he will realise their importance. Variations of this formula of alternative possibilities make up one of the most valuable resources of the poet.

Stanza 2:   . . . is most thoroughly ambiguous; there are two entirely different levels of meaning for the whole, and most of the parts exhibit a comparable stratification. I give a word-for-word analysis:

Do not expect me to be after death what I was alive and human:

the *fond* (1 *foolish*; 2 *loving* – you get the same two meanings in the synonym *doting*)

brisk (the normal meanings are favorable: *full of life, keenly alive or alert*: but here the context forces it over into *officious, undignified, solicitous, leaping at your every word* – there is a pathetic ignoble sense to it here)

lackey (the most contemptuous and degrading form of the word *servant*: a servile follower, a toady)

to fetch and carry (you thought so poorly of me that you let me perform nothing but silly menial physical tasks; thus, our love was nothing but the degrading relationship of obsequious servant and contemptuous master)

the true (1 *constant, loyal, devoted, faithful*; 2 *properly so-called, ideally or typically such* – the perfectly slavish slave)

sick-hearted (1 *cowardly, disheartened in a weak discouraged ignoble way*, as a Spartan would have said of helots, 'These sick-hearted slaves'; 2 sick at heart at the whole mess, his own helpless subjection. There was a man in one of the sagas who had a bad boil on his foot; when he was asked why he didn't limp and favor it, he replied: 'One walks straight while the leg is whole.' If the reader imagines this man as a slave he will see sharply the more elevated sense of the phrase *sick-hearted slave*)

slave (1 the conventional hardly meant sense in which we use it of lovers, as an almost completely dead metaphor: this sense has very little force here; or 2 the literal *slave*: the relation of slave to master is not pleasant, not honorable, is between lovers indecent and horrible, but immensely comprehensive – their love is made even more compulsive and even less favorable).

But here I leave the word-by-word analysis for more general comment. I think I hardly need remark on the shock in this treatment, which forces over the conventional unfelt terms into their literal degrading senses; and this shock is amplified by the paradoxical fall through *just city* and *free land* into *the grave*. (Also, the effect of the *lackey–carry* and versification of the first line of the stanza should be noted.)

Let me give first the favorable literal surface sense of *the just city and free land of the grave*, its sense on the level at which you take Housman's Greek underworld seriously. The house of

Hades is the *just city* for a number of reasons: in it are the three just judges; in it are all the exemplary convicts, from Ixion to the Danaides, simply dripping with justice; here justice is meted equally to the anonymous and rankless dead; there is no corruption here. It is the *free land* because here the king and the slave are equal (though even on the level of death as the Greek underworld, the horrid irony has begun to intrude – Achilles knew, and Housman knows, that it is better to be the slave of a poor farmer than king among the hosts of the dead); because here we are free at last from life; and so on and so on.

But at the deeper level, the *just* fastened to *city*, the *city* fastened to *grave*, have an irony that is thorough. How are we to apply *just* to a place where corruption and nothingness are forced on good and bad, innocent and guilty alike? (From Housman's point of view it might be called mercy, but never justice.) And the *city* is as bad; the cemetery looks like a city of the graves, of the stone rectangular houses – but a city without occupations, citizens, without life: a shell, a blank check that can never be filled out. And can we call a land *free* whose inhabitants cannot move a finger, are compelled as completely as stones? And can we call the little cave, the path of darkness and pressing earth, the *land* of the grave?

And why are we told to expect him not, the slave, the lackey, in the just city and free land of the grave? Because he is changed now, a citizen of the Greek underworld, engrossed in its games and occupations, the new interests that he has acquired? O no, the change is complete, not from the old interests to new ones, but from any interests to none; do not expect him because he has ceased to exist, he is really, finally different now. It is foolish to expect *anything* of the world after death. But we can expect nothingness; and that is better than this world, the poem is supposed to make us feel; there, even though we are overwhelmed impartially and completely, we shall be free of the evil of this world – a world whose best thing, love, is nothing but injustice and stupidity and slavery. This is why the poet resorts to the ambiguity that permits him to employ the adjectives *just* and *free*: they seem to apply truly on the surface level, and ironically at the other; but in a way they, and certainly the air of reward and luck and approbation that goes with them, apply truly at the second level as well. This is the accusation and condemnation of life that we read so often in Housman: that the grave seems better, we are glad to be in it.

We ought not to forget that this poem is a love-poem by the living 'me' of the poem to its equally living 'you': *when we are dead things will be different – and I'm glad of it.* It is, considerably sublimated, the formula familiar to such connections: *I wish I were dead*; and it has more than a suspicion of the child's *when I'm dead, then they'll be sorry.* It is an accusation that embodies a very strong statement of the underlying antagonism, the real ambivalence of most such relationships. The condemnation applied to the world for being bad is extended to the *you* for not being better. And these plaints are always pleas; so the poem has an additional force. Certainly this particular-seeming little poem turns out to be general enough: it carries implicit in it attitudes (aggregates of related generalisations) toward love, life, and death. . . .

SOURCE: extract from 'Texts from Housman', *Kenyon Review*, I (1939), pp. 261–6. [The close analysis of the first part of Stanza 2 has been revised in lay-out for this Casebook, for greater clarity – Ed.]

Donald Davie   'Syntax as Rhyme: T. S. Eliot'   (1955)

. . . For an example of [syntax as rhyme] in English, we can go to Eliot again, to the beginning of *Ash-Wednesday*:

1. Because I do not hope to turn again
2. Because I do not hope
3. Because I do not hope to turn
4. Desiring this man's gift and that man's scope

5.   I no longer strive to strive towards such things
6.   (Why should the aged eagle stretch its wings?)
7.   Why should I mourn
8.   The vanished power of the usual reign?
9.   Because I do not hope to know again
10.   The infirm glory of the positive hour
11.   Because I do not think
12.   Because I know I shall not know
13.   The one veritable transitory power
14.   Because I cannot drink
15.   There, where trees flower, and springs flow, for
      there is nothing again.

I have numbered these lines for ease of reference. Now if we compare lines 8, 10 and 13, it will be observed that 10 and 13 are tied together by an end-rhyme, but that 8 and 10 are tied together no less closely by similarity of grammar. What we have here, in fact, is a sort of parity of esteem between rhyme and metre and grammar or syntax. Every line in the second section, except for the last of all, 'rhymes' with some one or more lines in the first section. Thus 9 is linked with 8 by end-rhyme, but, as I have remarked, 10 no less 'rhymes' with 8 by virtue of grammar; 11 rhymes by syntax with 2; 12 rhymes with 3 by virtue of metre and a certain syntactical similarity, but also by syntax with 5 ('Know I shall not know' echoing 'strive to strive'); 13 rhymes through 10 with 8; and 14 rhymes, by metre and syntax, with 2. The two lines left over are 4 and 15, and one could even argue, though this might be straining a little, that these 'rhyme' together, simply by virtue of being each the odd one out (though each is linked by end-rhyme with another line in its own section).

This use of syntax as rhyme is certainly nearer to 'syntax like music' than to any of the other varieties so far considered. But I confess I am uncertain whether it does not constitute another category again . . . .

SOURCE: extract from *Articulate Energy: An Enquiry into the Syntax of English Poetry* (London, 1955), pp. 90–1.

Sylvère Monod 'The Vocabulary of *David Copperfield*' (1968)

. . . Dickens's use of language in *Copperfield* is characterised above all by the frequent recurrence of a number of words each of which corresponds to some aspect of his personality. In the first place, there are three adjectives whose significant repetition emphasises the author's sentimentality: 'little', 'own', and 'old'. 'Little' is constantly used by Dickens where another author might have used 'small.' His preference for this word, which has, according to the *Oxford Dictionary*, 'emotional implications not given by small', reveals his personal emotional approach to situations in a way that makes 'little' the most characteristic word in the whole Dickensian vocabulary. In a series of fourteen chapters – IX–XXIII – without taking into account the many occasions when Emily is called 'Little Em'ly', this favorite adjective occurs 186 times.[1] Its sentimental value is easily perceived. Within a single page of chapter IX, while David is in the shop of Mr Omer, the Yarmouth undertaker, shortly before Mrs Copperfield's burial, a moment when the atmosphere is supremely emotional, the word 'little' is used five times. David asks: 'Do you know how my little brother is, sir?' Then, on hearing that the child is in his mother's arms, in other words, dead, he exclaims: 'Oh, poor little fellow!' All so far is quite normal and in strict accordance with the traditional distinction between 'little' and 'small'. Yet emotion soon extends from persons to things and David speaks of the 'little room' in which he finds himself, of the 'little trip' which Minnie plans to take with her young man on the occasion of the funeral, and even of the 'little nails' – they are coffin nails, of course – which the workman keeps in his mouth.

The frequent recurrence of 'own' has a slightly different connotation. It is particularly striking in the Murdstone and Grinby episode, a passage of intense self-pity. In the same group of fourteen chapters as above there are eighty-five 'owns'. Most of them are applied by David to himself, often quite appropriately, but sometimes unnecessarily. Let us look at three examples from one page of chapter X: 'A solitary condition . . . apart from the society of all other boys of my own age, apart from all companionship but my own spiritless thoughts', and 'A little small light-haired wife, whom I can just remember connecting in my own thoughts with a pale tortoise-shell cat'. The first two are legitimate, as their function is clearly to oppose David's solitude to the normal outside world, but the third could have been dispensed with. There is even something morbid in David's way of emphasising the privacy of his thinking.

'Own' is occasionally employed by other characters, such as Mr Murdstone, who is of course not sentimental, but who is intensely proud, with similar results: 'I have my own opinion . . . founded . . . in part on my knowledge of my own means and resources. . . . I place this boy under the eye of a friend of my own, in a respectable business', he tells Miss Betsey, who then retorts: 'About the respectable business . . . if he had been your own boy, you would have put him to it, just the same, I suppose!' And Miss Murdstone cuts in with: 'If he had been my brother's own boy . . . his character, I trust, would have been altogether different' [ch. XIV].

A complete examination of Dickens's sentimental vocabulary in *Copperfield* ought to deal with the emotional use of 'poor' and 'miserable', but they are not of comparable importance to the third favorite – 'old'. In chapters XI–XXI, 'old' occurs ninety-seven times. Dickens's liking for that adjective is striking and he almost invariably uses it in the emotional sense of 'familiar' rather than in the primary sense of 'not young'. This is not surprising in a novel written under the influence of sincere and vivid emotion and in which sentimental complacency in the contemplation of the past imparts to whatever belongs to former days – to the time 'of old', – an irresistible charm. There are numerous examples of this attitude in *Copperfield*. Speaking to David of his young, dead mother, Peggotty says: 'The last time that I saw her like her own old self was the night when you came home, my dear

. . .' [ch. IX]. Here the combination of the two keywords 'own' and 'old' is the sure sign of an emotional crisis, like the combination of 'old' and 'little' in a tender description of Little Em'ly: 'She sat, at this time, and all the evening, on the old locker, in her old little corner by the fire' [ch. XXI]. At the end of the novel, when David, now a widower, sees Agnes again in her home after three years' separation, she tells him: 'Here are the old books, Trotwood, and the old music' to which he replies: 'Even the old flowers are here . . . or the old kinds' [ch. LX]. Dickens's fondness for the word is such that, even when he uses it in its primary sense, he cannot help presenting it in an amiable light. David, for instance, is immediately under the spell of Mr Wickfield's home, where everything is old: 'the quaint little panes of glass and quainter little windows . . . as old as the hills'; 'the tall old chimney-piece'; 'a wonderful old staircase'; 'old oak seats'; 'all old nooks and corners'; 'a glorious old room' [ch. XV].

Besides his sentimental tendency, many other aspects of Dickens's character are illuminated by the study of his vocabulary. His natural intensity is clearly revealed by words like 'quite', 'great', 'indeed', by the phrase 'a good' – or 'a great' – 'deal', and by the presence of numerous superlatives and other forms of reinforcement. 'Quite' appears eighty-nine times in chapters IX–XXI, and that adverb is called upon to intensify a wide variety of adjectives throughout the narrative. Its frequency is strikingly great in the Yarmouth scenes, which shows its implicit connection with his sentimental vocabulary. It is first found in chapter III – 'I Have a Change' on David's first visit to Mr Peggotty's – and in that single chapter occur the following expressions: 'I was quite tired'; 'the counterpane made my eyes quite ache'; 'you're quite a sailor'; 'I felt it difficult to picture him quite at his ease'; 'I hardly know enough of the race . . . to be quite certain'; 'I am sure I loved that baby quite as truly, quite as tenderly'; 'I did not quite understand'; ' "Peggotty!" said I, quite frightened'; 'I knew quite well that he was looking at us both'. Within eight chapters – XIV–XXII – are to be found thirty uses of 'indeed', most frequently in the characters' speeches. Uriah Heep, in his constant fawning and in his desire to be persuasive, is a great wielder of 'indeed'. The slightly childish 'a good deal' and 'a good many' for 'much' or 'many' also crop up often. Finally, in the intensifying vocabulary, the first place is occupied by 'great', which appears as the counterpart of 'little'. The difference between 'great' and 'big' or 'large' is said, by the *Oxford Dictionary* again, to be that 'great' is employed 'usually with implied surprise, contempt, indignation, etc.' so that Dickens's preference once more goes to the more sentimental English word. In chapters XI–XXI, 'great' occurs eighty-five times.

Intensity is expressed in other ways also. The superlative recurs so often in *David Copperfield* that there can hardly be a single emotion not experienced by the hero in its supreme degree, or a single kind of sight not seen by him in its most representative form. In the quotations that follow, it will often be observed that the superlative is itself reinforced and intensified by 'ever' or 'never'. Of the old clothes dealer in Chatham, David says: 'There never was such another drunken madman in this line of business' [ch. XIII], and to him the laid up Barkis 'looked the queerest object I ever beheld' [ch. XXI]; yet when Miss Mowcher appeared, 'I never did in my days behold anything like Miss Mowcher' [ch. XXII]. 'In my days' does not add perceptibly to the meaning and is only a way of reinforcing and intensifying the expression. David meets with a fierce-looking milkman: 'As to his dealing in the mild article of milk . . . there never was a greater anomaly' [ch. XXVII]. Of Mrs Crupp he tells us: 'I never was so much afraid of anyone' [ch. XXVIII]. Miss Dartle's song is 'the most unearthly I have ever heard in my life, or can imagine' [ch. XXIX], in which 'in my life' – like 'in my days' of the previous quotation – and perhaps 'or can imagine' add very little to the sense of an expression which really means: Miss Dartle's song was very unearthly. Of Miss Betsey, her nephew writes, 'I believe there never was anybody with such an imperturbable countenance when she chose' [ch. XXXV]; of Mr Micawber: 'I never saw a man so thoroughly enjoy himself . . . as Mr Micawber did that afternoon' [ch. XXVIII]; and of Mr Micawber's culinary masterpiece, one page later, 'There never was a greater success'. When Agnes and Dora become acquainted: 'I never was so happy. I never was so pleased as when I saw those two sit down together' [ch. XLII]. Within a single page of the melodramatic scene on the bank of the Thames with Martha Endell occur two superlative notes: 'I have never known what despair was, except in the tone of those words. . . . I never saw, in any painting or reality, horror and compassion so impressively blended' [ch. XLVII], and again after the departure of the emigrants' ship: 'A sight at once so beautiful, so mournful and so hopeful . . . I never saw' [ch. LVII]. David makes the acquaintance of young Mrs Traddles and concludes: 'A more cheerful, amiable, honest, happy, bright-looking bride, I believe . . . the world never saw' [ch. LIX].

When they are thus accumulated, such vigorous expressions destroy one another's effect. When the characters' whole emotional life goes on in the superlative degree, there occurs a downward levelling of all emotion. The author's fondness for strong expressions is shown explicitly in a fragment of conversation between the hero and Littimer, who says:

'Mr Steerforth will be glad to hear how you have rested, sir.' 'Thank you', said I, 'very well indeed. Is Mr Steerforth quite well?' 'Thank you, sir, Mr Steerforth is tolerably well.' Another of his characteristics. No use of superlatives. A cool calm medium always. [ch. XVI]

It will be observed that the contrast between David-Dickens' warm words ('very well indeed', 'quite well') and the servant's prudent coolness ('tolerably well') does not seem sufficiently clear to the author. He must emphasise the point: 'No use of superlatives.' Mildness of speech is a serious, unforgivable offence. It is hardly an exaggeration to say that the absence of superlatives, the cold, calculating reticence, and the lack of impulse and passion already betray the criminal in Littimer and foreshadow his later imprisonment. Dickens will not have 'a cool calm medium', or certainly not 'always'.

Now and then, however, Dickens would realise the potential danger in his excessive fondness for intense and energetic expressions and use such terms as 'almost', 'nearly', and 'hardly ever,' (instead of 'never') in order to tone down the effect of being too categorical in his assertions. The use of extenuating phrases even becomes a secondary, though perceptible, characteristic of his style. Within a few pages, in chapters X and XI, an imposing series can be found: 'so squeezed that I could hardly bear it'; 'until the breath was nearly wedged out of me'; 'he . . . almost choked her'; '[Steerforth] will give you almost as many men as you like at draughts, and beat you easily'; 'I have almost lost the capacity of being much surprised by anything'; 'I hardly ever . . . saw both the twins detached from Mrs Micawber at the same time'.

Still, Dickens's tendency to use and even abuse reinforcing adverbs is very pronounced – they will often miss their aim when they are applied to terms intrinsically energetic. The tendency is perceptible in Dickens's letters, always written in a highly tense style, and also in *Copperfield*, especially, it would seem, when his self-control is relaxed and he lapses into his most spontaneous, least elaborate modes of expression. Words like 'heartbroken', 'dejected', 'angelic', 'luxurious', 'wretched and miserable', 'atrocious'. 'worn out', 'dreadful', 'assuredly', 'terror', 'elated', 'amazing', and 'appalling', are undoubtedly among the most energetic in the English language. For this reason, any attempt at further intensifying them can only detract from their vigour, since it amounts to treating them like ordinary adjectives and disguising their distinctive force. Yet that is just what Dickens does when he writes: 'quite heart-broken', 'greatly dejected'; 'perfectly angelic'; 'a very luxurious state of mind'; 'a very wretched and miserable condition'; 'a most atrocious criminal'; 'quite worn out'; 'the most dreadful manner'; 'perfectly miserable'; 'most assuredly'; 'infinite terror'; 'greatly elated'; 'most amazing'; 'most appalling'.[2]

Another kind of levelling can be achieved through a less close juxtaposition. For instance, when the adverbs 'exquisitely', 'utterly', and 'perfectly' are all three used in one and the same paragraph [ch. XI], or within a few lines of each other, one finds the following expressions: 'in a most distrustful manner'; 'such extreme joy', 'a very unmelodious laugh'; and 'a most delicious meal' [ch. V], an impression of uniformity is created, instead of the impression of high relief that Dickens was aiming at in each case.

The remarkable and sustained vigor of expression in Dickens's style is accompanied by a curious hesitancy which nothing in his character seems to suggest, but which is revealed by the recurrence of the phrases 'a kind of' or 'a sort of'. Dickens's thinking and creative vision were vague or blurred very little, yet the text of *Copperfield* leaves no doubt about the existence of the opposite tendency. In chapters IX–XXI, the two phrases are employed no fewer than seventy-seven times. This may result from an attempt at compensating for the excessive trenchancy to be found more often. Or it may be due to the author's desire to produce, by dint of apparent scrupulousness, a greater sense of truth, again in connection with the autobiographical character of the work. But, as the frequency of such forms is hardly less in Dickens's other novels, it is more probable that the main cause for this phenomenon lies in Dickens's liking for approximate illustration and simile. Dickens was aware that the proliferation of 'a sort of' or 'a kind of' was mainly characteristic of unintellectual and uncultivated persons. His awareness is shown by the implicit criticism contained in the awkward speech of men like Mr Omer – 'By that sort of thing we very often lose a little mint of money' [ch. IX] – or the coachman who takes David from Canterbury to London. Yet David's own frequent use of these phrases is not of decidedly higher quality. Almost invariably, 'sort of' or 'kind of' could be cancelled without suppressing anything except an element of unprofitable inaccuracy: 'it made no sort of difference in her'; 'he carried a jaunty sort of a stick'; 'he was a sort of a town traveller'; 'a sort of grass-grown battery'; 'in a sort of tune'; 'with every sort of expression but wonder'; 'with a strange kind of watery brightness'.[3]

To bring to a close the list of the external, though significant aspects of Dickens's language in *Copperfield*, a word should be said of the stage directions with which the speeches of the characters are interspersed. It will be observed that he usually designates the author of each speech with great care. It is very seldom that a phrase, however brief, and even when it occurs unequivocally in dialogue, is mentioned without some specific reference to its origin. Almost invariably, there is at least a 'said he' after the speech. Nor is there much variety in that respect. Sometimes, in the longer speeches, a second 'said he' or an 'added he' is inserted at or near the end, but the predominance of 'said' over all the other verbs that can be similarly used is overwhelming. In chapters XVI–XVIII, for instance, are to be found the following verbs: 'asked' ten times and 'inquired' twice, but 'said' is often used after an interrogation in the sense of 'asked'; 'returned' twenty-one times; 'answered' four times; 'replied' six times; 'retorted' three times; 'exclaimed' three times; 'observed' twice; 'interposed' once; 'pursued' and 'repeated' three times each; 'continued' and 'hinted' once each; while 'said' occurs ninety-three times. Only nineteen speeches are given without any verb. These rarely exceed a word or two – 'Shall I?' 'Certainly', 'Yes, sir' – and when they occur in rapid conversation, they can be completed by a genuine stage direction without a verb, for instance, 'with astonishment'. Finally, within speeches already introduced by 'he said' are to be found one 'he added' and eleven repetitions of 'he said'.

The clear predominance of 'said' shows that Dickens does not take much interest in this particular aspect of the presentation of dialogue. He is often bordering on theatrical writing, in which information of this kind has no place, while the suggestion of gestures and emotions plays a great part. This is precisely what happens in *Copperfield*. One can take a conversation from that novel almost at random, and the results will always be the same. For example, in the case of the brief interview between David and Steerforth in a London hotel [ch. XIX], there are many stage directions:

I looked at him . . . but I saw no recognition in his face. . . . I grasped him by both hands, and could not let them go. . . . shaking my hands heartily. . . . I brushed away the tears. . . . I made a clumsy laugh of it, and we sat down together, side by side. . . . clapping me on the shoulder. . . . He laughed as he ran his hand through the clustering curls of his hair, and said gaily. . . . Steerforth laughed heartily . . . clapping me on the shoulder again . . . 'Holloa, you, sir!' this was addressed to the waiter who had been very attentive to our recognition at a distance, and now came forward deferentially. . . . the waiter with an apologetic air. . . . the waiter, still apologetically.

Every detail is described and the reader can visualise the scene as though he were seeing it performed in a theatre. The amount of attention bestowed by Dickens on gestures and attitudes is almost greater than his interest in the words spoken by the characters. His passionate attraction to the stage and the influence it had on his fictional art are made perceptible in such passages, which also confirm the somewhat visual and external rather than analytical nature of his approach to psychology and characterisation.

Dickens's style in the days of *Copperfield* is much more distinctly his own than it had been at the time of *Sketches by Boz*. The words, phrases and devices studied in the foregoing paragraphs ought to make a page by Dickens easily identifiable. And the habits concerned are, by the time of *Copperfield*, so ingrained that, with minor variations, they endure to the end of his career.

SOURCE: extract from *Dickens the Novelist* (Norman, Oklahoma, 1968), pp. 335–43; previously published in French as *Dickens romancier* (Paris, 1953).

NOTES

1. Most of the figures mentioned in the following paragraphs concern that section of the novel.

2. Chapters II, III, IV, V, X, XIV, XXII, LV. In *Sketches by Boz* were already to be found the forms 'the most hopeless extreme' ('Scenes', ch. XI); 'perfectly astonishing' ('Scenes', ch. IX); 'most striking' ('Scenes', ch. I); 'a perfectly wild state' ('Tales', Bk. 1, ch. II); 'most inimitably' ('Tales', ch. XI); and, in the famous letter about *Oliver Twist*, 'indispensably necessary' ('Tales', ch. XII).

3. Chapters X, XI, XIII.

Vernon Lee   'The Language of Tess of the d'Urbervilles' (1923)

[The author begins by quoting a passage from chapter XVI of Hardy's novel.]

However, Tess found at least approximate expression for her feelings in the old *Benedicite* that she had lisped from infancy; and it was enough. Such high contentment with such a slight initial performance as that of having started towards a means of independent living was a part of the Durbeyfield temperament. Tess really wished to walk uprightly, while her father did nothing of the kind; but she resembled him in being content with immediate and small achievements, and in having no mind for laborious effort towards such petty social advancement as could alone be effected by a family so heavily handicapped as the once powerful d'Urbervilles were now.

There was, it might be said, the energy of her mother's unexpended family, as well as the natural energy of Tess's years, rekindled after the experience which had so overwhelmed her for the time. Let the truth be told – women do as a rule live through such humiliations, and regain their spirits, and again look about them with an interested eye. While there's life there's hope is a conviction not so entirely unknown to the 'betrayed' as some amiable theorists would have us believe.

Tess Durbeyfield, then, in good heart, and full of zest for life, descended the Egdon slopes lower and lower towards the dairy of her pilgrimage.

The marked difference, in the final particular, between the rival vales now showed itself. The secret of Blackmoor was best discovered from the heights around; to read aright the valley before her it was necessary to descend into its midst. When Tess had accomplished this feat she found herself to be standing on a carpeted level, which stretched to the east and west as far as the eye could reach.

The river had stolen from the higher tracts and brought in particles to the vale all this horizontal land; and now, exhausted, aged, and attenuated, lay serpentining along through the midst of its former spoils.

Not quite sure of her direction Tess stood still upon the hemmed expanse of verdant flatness, like a fly on a billiard table of indefinite length, and of no more consequence to the surroundings than that fly. The sole effect of her presence upon the placid valley so far had been to excite the mind of a solitary heron, which, after descending to the ground not far from her path, stood with neck erect, looking at her.

Suddenly there arose from all parts of the lowland a prolonged and repeated call –

'Waow! waow! waow!'

From the furthest east to the furthest west the cries spread by contagion, accompanied in some cases by the barking of a dog. It was not the expression of the valley's consciousness that beautiful Tess had arrived, but the ordinary announcement of milking-time – half-past four o'clock, when the dairy men set about getting in the cows.

This passage forces me to examine into the nature of the words I have counted in my several analyses. For whereas the other Writers analysed give from 132 to 159 nouns, Hardy gives 108; while verbs rise to 62, higher, that is, than Kipling and Hewlett, and adjectives to 62; that is to say 9 more than Kipling, 8 more than Hewlett, who was highest on my list. First let me see how I account for those additional adjectives.

At first sight, on re-reading the passage from end to end, I am not struck by many adjectives and adverbs to omit. It does perhaps seem unnecessary that the river should be both 'exhausted, aged, and attenuated'. But on reconsidering the sentence it is difficult to decide which of these adjectives is the superfluous one. *Exhausted* is not implied in attenuated, nor is either *exhausted* or *attenuated* implied in *aged*, nor *aged* in the two others. The expression tallies with the thought; and it is the thought itself which is redundant and vague. We are being *told all about* the locality, not what is necessary for the intelligence of the situation. For instance, in these five hundred words we are twice given points of the compass – that is to say, information which has nothing to do with the subject in hand, and which the Reader neither needs, nor, as a fact, is able to apply. Since points of the compass can add to the meaning of a passage only if: (1) We already possess the geography of the region, and require to feel in which direction on the map the traveller is going; thus it is of consequence to know that Stevenson drove his donkey, say, south-east or south-west; it is of consequence if I say, 'forests lying north of Paris' or 'the seaboard west of Rome', etc. (2) Points of the compass can be mentioned to some purpose if they imply a peculiarity of light or warmth or the time of day; we learn something when we are told that 'the sun was now in the west', or that a room 'faces north'.

But what do we learn when Hardy tells us that a particular valley, whose name is imaginary, *stretched to the east and west as far as the eye could reach.* The only movement in one's mind is a faint question, 'Was the valley so very narrow as not to stretch at all north and south; and, if it was so narrow, is the word *stretched* very applicable to its east and west direction?

We get a reference to this detail of orientation further on – 'from the furthest east to the furthest west the cries spread' – and, since we perceive no reason for this dragging in of points of the compass, we imagine one, and get a vague idea that the sounds rose in the east in some sort of connection with the sun. At least this is my experience; and I feel annoyed at finding that that east and west really implies nothing about the sounds.

I therefore suspect that all this talk of orientation is a mere mark of irrelevant writing, of saying everything there is to be said about the subject, as we have seen about the river. It is a soliloquy of Hardy's about two valleys and their contents, without reference to the story or the Reader. Listen to him! 'The marked difference, in the final particular, between the rival vales, now showed itself' – 'The secret of Blackmoor was best discovered from the heights around; to read aright the valley before her it was necessary to descend into its midst.'

Now, we can quite imagine a passage in Stevenson comparing two valleys much in this manner; but then the valleys and his journey, the genius of the place, so to speak, would be the chief personages; and the points of comparison would be such as the Reader, who had never been in that neighbourhood, could visualise in fancy. But here we are not merely listening to Hardy's recollections poured out without reference to us, but we are, while doing so, interrupted in our attempt to follow the adventures and the inner vicissitudes of Tess. All this detail about the geological formation, 'the river had stolen from the higher tracts and brought in particles to the vale all this horizontal land' – all this orientation and comparison of lie of land is subject to the sentence: 'Tess Durbeyfield then . . . full of zest for life, descended the Egdon slopes lower and lower towards the dairy of her pilgrimage.' And the sentence of comparison between the two valleys is suddenly succeeded by 'when Tess had accomplished this feat she found herself to be standing on a green-carpeted level', etc.

After which we again leave Tess in order to remark on the geological history, as noted above.

After disposing of the river in the prehistoric past, we revert to Tess, who 'was not quite sure of her direction'. And this lack of certainty is in Hardy as well as in his heroine.

Notice how he tells us the very simple fact of how Tess stops to look round: 'Tess . . . stood still upon the hemmed expanse of verdant flatness, like a fly on a billiard-table of indefinite length'. '*Hemmed* expanse', that implies that the expanse had limits; it is, however, compared to a billiard-table 'of indefinite length'. Hardy's attention has slackened, and really he is talking a little at random. If he visualised that valley, particularly from above, he would not think of it, which is bounded by something on his own higher level (*hemmed*, by which he means *hemmed in*), in connection with a billiard-table which is bounded by the tiny wall of its cushion. I venture to add that if, at the instant of writing, he were feeling the variety, the freshness of a valley, he would not be comparing it to a piece of cloth, with which it has only two things in common: being flat and being green; the utterly dissimilar flatness and greenness of a landscape and that of a billiard-table.

We are surely in presence of slackened interest when the Writer casts about for and accepts any illustration, without realising it sufficiently to reject it. Such slackening of attention is confirmed by the poor structure of the sentence, 'a fly on a billiard-table of indefinite length *and* of no more consequence to the surroundings than that fly'. The *and* refers the 'of no more consequence' in the first instance to the billiard-table. Moroever, I venture to think that the whole remark was not worth making: why divert our attention from Tess and her big, flat valley, surely easy enough to realise, by a vision of a billiard-table with a fly on it? Can the two images ever grow into one another? is the first made clearer, richer, by the second? How useless all this business has been is shown by the next sentence: 'The sole effect of her presence upon the placid valley so far had been to excite the mind of a solitary heron, which, after descending to the ground not far from her path, stood, with neck erect, looking at her.'

Leave out all about the billiard-table, and the sentences coalesce perfectly and give us all we care to know. Such as Hardy has left them they give us a good deal more; not indeed of items, but of words. 'The *sole effect* of her *presence*,' etc. Here are two nouns, both abstract, and an adjective not of quality but degree. Then 'so far' – with the tense 'had been' – giving the notion of far longer time than Tess probably stayed looking about. Moreover, her presence excited not the solitary heron, but the *mind* of the solitary heron. And the heron, we are told, 'descended to the ground *not far* (why not *near*?) from her path', etc. How all the action of the heron's downward flight and sudden inquisitive stopping is lost in all these circuitous phrases! We scarcely see the heron at all.

After all these meanderings the next sentence fairly startles us, and since it tells us of something startling it is right it should startle us. But it does so merely by contrast with the vagueness of the preceding sentences: for in itself it is weak and vague. 'Suddenly there arose . . . a call' is the only active element in it; '*from all parts* of the lowland' is again feeble, for the meaning is simply 'from all around', and the reference to *parts*, the reiteration of *lowlands* (as if by this time we hadn't been told often enough that we were in a valley!) is mere padding.

The next sentence is largely a repetition of this, with the added and useless orientation, 'from the furthest east to the furthest west – the cries spread'. But Hardy must needs add 'as if by contagion'. This adds something, undoubtedly, to the meaning; but the idyllic impression of the pastoral cries waking each other as they spread does not gain by suggesting the spread of a malady! Nor is Hardy even now satisfied: 'accompanied *in some cases* by the barking of a dog'. He has given us an orientation, he has explained that the cries arose in echoing succession; why bring in 'some cases', why say 'accompanied by', when the meaning is simply 'and here and there the bark of a dog'?

But Hardy has started on further and even less necessary information, for he tells us: 'It was not the expression of the valley's consciousness that beautiful Tess had arrived' – who in his senses would have thought that it was? Meanwhile we have got two abstractions and a personification, in a cumbersome attempt to weld together the disjointed items about the valley's origin (old exhausted stream), its orientation, flatness, greenness, billiard-table, etc., with Tess's journey. I can only surmise that Hardy has become suddenly aware of having left Tess in the lurch and wants to make up for it. Then he is afraid lest we should take this poetico-mythological 'expression' of the valley's consciousness too seriously. It wasn't that in the very least, he hastens to tell us, it was 'but the ordinary announcement of milking-time', and he adds 'half-past four o'clock, when the dairymen set about getting in the cows'.

This page is so constructed, or rather not constructed, that if you skip one sentence, you are pretty sure to receive the same information in the next; and if you skip both, you have a chance of hearing all you need later on. This makes it lazy reading; and it is lazy writing. . . .

SOURCE: extract from *The Handling of Words* (London, 1923), pp. 224–30.

Derek Bickerton   The Language of *Women in Love*   (1967)

While Lawrence's high status as a novelist is now widely accepted, there is still room for a considerable measure of disagreement about the quality of his actual writing. To Professor Leavis, he is 'plainly one of the greatest masters of what is certainly one of the greatest languages'.[1] To T. S. Eliot, on the other hand, 'he seems often to write very badly, but to be a writer who had to write often badly in order to write sometimes well'.[2] An American critic, John McCormick, takes an intermediate view: 'That Lawrence was capable of writing superb prose is obvious from most of his short stories, occasional moments in *Sons and Lovers*, *The Rainbow*, *St Mawr*, and some of the other novels . . . But too often, particularly in his later novels, he relied on the devices of repetition, rhythm and the catalogue to create incantation.'[3]

Widely differing concepts of 'a writer' and 'good writing' may be at issue here; however, texts which can give rise to such fundamental differences of opinion clearly require a closer scrutiny than they have so far received.

To discuss Lawrence's prose as a whole is beyond the scope of a brief paper. All I propose to do is to examine one particular novel, to see whether certain features of the language therein displayed can be in any way related to the feeling of vague unease which some readers have derived from it.

I have chosen to concentrate on *Women in Love* for two further reasons. In the first place, many critics accept it as being probably Lawrence's greatest novel, 'incredibly rich in detail and dense in substance',[4] one of the half-dozen most important novels of the present century'[5] – even as 'one of the most striking works of creative originality that fiction has to show'.[6] Clearly any criticism of Lawrence's writing should aim at his strongest rather than his weakest point; it would be too easy, and quite pointless, to cull an anthology of *bétises* from one who wrote as much, and as quickly, as he did. Secondly, Lawrence himself realised there was something unusual about the language of *Women in Love*. It was his declared intention to go 'a stratum deeper than I think anybody has ever gone, in a novel',[7] and, by abandoning the 'old stable ego of the character', to lay bare 'another ego, according to whose action the individual is unrecognisable, and passes through, as it were, allotropic states which it needs a deeper sense than any we've been used to exercise, to discover are states of the same single radically unchanged element'.[8] He wished, in other words, to work at a level deeper than that of everyday consciousness, and quickly came to the conclusion that the 'hard, violent style full of sensation and presentation',[9] in which he had written *Sons and Lovers*, was not adaptable for this purpose. As early as January 1913 he had admitted that his projected novel *The Sisters* – from which both *The Rainbow* and *Women in Love* were subsequently derived – was 'far less visualised'; a little later he wrote: 'I am doing a novel which I have never grasped . . . it's like a novel in a foreign language I don't know very well – I can only just make out what it's about.'[10]

Though no one has ever analysed this 'foreign language', even Lawrence's admirers have felt some reservations about it. Graham Hough admits that on occasions the style 'lapses into inflation and bathos';[11] Professor Leavis, after quoting a passage from chapter 33 ('Excurse'), points out the presence of 'something one can only call jargon', a jargon he defines as 'an insistent and over-emphatic explicitness'. He describes this, however, as 'a fault that I do not now see as bulking so large in the book as I used to see it'.[12]

Large or not, 'explicitness' seems hardly the word for it. Part of the passage Professor Leavis quotes goes as follows:

> He felt as if he were seated in immemorial potency, like the great carven statues of real Egypt, as real and fulfilled with subtle strength as these are, with a vague inscrutable smile on their lips. He knew what it was to have the strange and magical current of force in his back and loins, and down his legs, force so perfect that it stayed him immobile, and left his face subtly, mindlessly smiling. He knew what it was to be awake and potent in the other basic mind, the deepest physical control, magical, mystical, a force in darkness, like electricity.[13]

Far from being 'explicit', this seems an attempt to inflate a perfectly ordinary situation – that of a man driving in a car with a woman to whom he is about to make love – into an experience of supra-normal significance, by an accumulation of highly emotive but almost meaningless adjectives: 'immemorial', 'subtle', 'vague', 'inscrutable', 'strange', 'perfect', 'magical' (twice), 'mystical'. In the words of a distinguished critic:

> Hadn't he, we find ourselves asking, overworked 'inscrutable', 'inconceivable', 'unspeakable', and that kind of word already? – yet still they recur . . . The same vocabulary, the same adjectival insistence upon inexpressible and incomprehensible mystery, is applied to the evocation of human profundities and spiritual horrors; to magnifying a thrilled sense of the unspeakable potentialities of the human soul. The actual effect is not to magnify but rather to muffle.

The critic is Professor Leavis himself; he happens, however, to be discussing, not Lawrence, but Conrad.[14] Yet, for reasons unexplained, the same fault that 'mars' *Heart of Darkness* does not 'bulk large' in *Women in Love*; what is sauce for the Polish goose is obviously not sauce for the Nottingham gander.

Since Professor Leavis himself admits that he 'could find worse examples in *Women in Love*', no purpose is to be served by further quotation; the more important question we now have to consider is whether this 'jargon' can be dismissed, as he and Mr Hough dismiss it, as an occasional and trivial blemish, or whether it is merely the most obvious symptom of a malady which penetrates the entire work.

Attention was drawn, in the passage just quoted, to a striking disproportion between language and content; and this disproportion, and the straining after effect which goes with it, is not limited to passages which can be dismissed as jargon. Sometimes it shows itself clearly in the passages of 'bathos' which Mr Hough noted:

But the next day, she did not come, she sent a note that she was kept indoors by a cold. Here was a torment![15]

But more often one must jerk one's own mind back to the situational context to realise how far the intensity of the language exceeds normal expectations.

A terrible storm came over her, as if she were drowning. She was possessed by a devastating hopelessness . . . Never had she known such a pang of utter and final hopelessness. It was beyond death, so utterly null, desert.[16]

(Hermione Roddice, at the Crich-Lupton wedding, has just noticed that her lover Birkin has not yet arrived; he does, a few moments later.)

'Ursula!' cried Gudrun. 'Isn't it amazing? Can you believe you lived in this place and never felt it? How I lived here a day without dying of terror, I cannot conceive!'[17]

(The Brangwen sisters are revisiting the perfectly ordinary house from which their family has just moved after living there uneventfully for many years.)

'Unless something happens', she said to herself, in the perfect lucidity of final suffering, 'I shall die. I am at the end of my line of life' . . . . In a kind of spiritual trance, she yielded, she gave way, and all was dark.[18]

(Ursula, waiting at home for Birkin to call, has concluded he is not coming: again, he does arrive shortly afterwards.)

These are random examples, which could be multiplied indefinitely. The result of this use, or abuse, of language is twofold: its effect on the reader is 'not to magnify, but rather to muffle'; and, when Lawrence has to deal with a scene of genuine emotional violence, such as the quarrel between Ursula and Birkin which precedes their final coming-together, he has so debased his lexical currency that he has nothing left but novelettish cliché:

Suddenly a flame ran over her, and she stamped her foot madly on the ground, and he winced . . . . Her brows knitted, her eyes blazed like a tiger's.[19]

The muffling and blurring effect produced by this persistent inflation is augmented by Lawrence's peculiar, and peculiarly frequent, use of certain words and phrases. To demonstrate this, I shall be obliged to resort to statistical counts, a method in some disfavour nowadays, owing to its indiscriminate use; however, no other means will show in a small compass the extent of practices which, in specific contexts and to a limited degree, might be justifiable enough, but which, in bulk, amount to a vice of style.

For example, certain key words are used in such a way that they lose their normal meaning. 'Torture' and 'torment' occur a total of thirty-nine times in the text, although (if we except Gerald's treatment of his mare, which accounts for only two occurrences) no scenes of physical torture are described or even mentioned. In a fifteen-hundred word passage at the beginning of chapter 15, the words 'death', 'die', 'dead' are used a total of forty-five times (although no actual death occurs), and the words 'life', 'live', 'living' twenty-four times. Whether or not we agree with Sweeney that 'Death is life and life is death', the effect of such a passage is to render the terms virtually indistinguishable.

Still more remarkable is Lawrence's use of two groups of

words, one of which serves merely to intensify, the other to convey indecision and vagueness.[20]

In the first I include 'very' (185 occurrences), 'so' used as an adverb of degree, i.e. 'so utterly null' (155), 'really' (79), 'complete/completely' (63), and 'utter/utterly' (37). Several words which have scarcely more lexical force are employed as frequently, 'perfect/perfectly' (170 times), 'pure/ purely' (127), 'terrible/terribly' (64), 'awful' (21) and 'dreadful' (15).

In the second group, we find what might be called the 'structure-words of vagueness', 'as if' (282 times), 'almost' (191), 'rather' (106), the indefinite 'some' – as in 'she seemed wrapped in some glittering abstraction' (115) – 'a certain' (49), 'a little' as adverb of degree (43), 'sort of' (50), 'kind of' (17) and 'perhaps' (31). Similar to these is 'strange/strangely', used in the sense of 'out of the ordinary, hard to define' rather than that of 'previously unknown'. This item occurs 257 times, and the synonymous uses of 'curious/curiously', 'odd/oddly', 'queer/queerly', 'uncanny/uncannily' provide a further 137 items. The verb 'seem' is used 301 times; 'slight/slightly', 80; 'faint/faintly' 58; 'vague/vaguely', 38. 'Quite' seems to straddle both groups; in a sentence such as 'There had been some discussion, on the whole quite intellectual and artificial', are we to assume that the discussion was *rather* intellectual, or *completely* intellectual? Anyway, it occurs 97 times.

Granted, these are all words a writer has to use at some time or other; but in *Women in Love*, which contains (excluding dialogue) roughly 150,000 words, they add up to a total of 2,768 – that is to say, they account for nearly one word in every fifty. They are not, of course, evenly distributed. Sometimes their impact is negligible, though not a page is entirely free of them. But where they are densely clotted, their effect is striking: a single example will have to suffice:

He [Gerald] *seemed* to stand with a proper, rich weight on the face of the earth, whilst Birkin *seemed* to have the centre of gravitation in his own middle. And Gerald had a rich, frictional *kind of* strength, *rather* mechanical, but sudden and invincible, whereas Birkin was *abstract* as to be *almost intangible*. He impinged *invisibly* upon the other man, *scarcely seeming* to touch him, like a garment, and then suddenly piercing in a tense fine grip that *seemed* to penetrate into the *very* quick of Gerald's being.[21]

There are four 'as ifs', three 'seems', three 'stranges', three indefinite 'somes', one 'almost', one 'scarcely', one 'kind of' and one 'uncanny' in the three shortish paragraphs that follow. The effect is that of a man trying, by qualification, to pass off as sense something which, if stated unequivocally, would come perilously close to nonsense. The extract is from the description of the Crich-Birkin wrestling match. Several critics have speculated inconclusively on whether we are to attach a homosexual significance to this scene; not one that I have read has connected his failure with the imprecision of the language in which the episode is described.

All the stylistic features so far mentioned could certainly be attributed to the fact that Lawrence is 'uncertain of the value of what he offers; uncertain whether he really holds it'[22] – an uncertainty which may now appear far more extensive than Professor Leavis admits. Other features are less easily explicable. That of repetition has been frequently noted, though it has never been analysed in detail. Here we have Lawrence's own explanation:

Fault is often found with the continual, slightly modified repetition. The only answer is that it is natural to the author, and that every natural crisis in emotion or passion or understanding comes from this pulsing, frictional to-and-fro which works up to culmination.[23]

This just will not do. Even if we accept his definition of 'natural crises' – which sounds more like a description of another of his favourite subjects – we need not accept the 'fallacy of expressive form' which is implicit in his statement. To mirror an actual process in style is not necessarily the best way of expressing it; a writer who couches, say, the boredom of his characters in a prose of deliberate monotony will only succeed in boring and repelling the reader. And to say that repetition 'is natural to the author' is not true; up to and including *Sons and Lovers*, it forms a negligible element in Lawrence's prose. It begins to make itself felt in *The Rainbow*; by the final version of *Women in Love*, it is no longer confined to 'natural crises', it has begun to pervade even passages of straightforward description. It is not sufficient to say simply that the air in the Alps was cold; 'it was so terribly cold . . . it was indeed cold, bruisingly, frighteningly, unnaturally cold . . . it seemed conscious, malevolent, purposive in its intense murderous coldness'.[24] (These three sentences occur within eight lines.)

Similarly, the 'code-words' which are attached to several of the characters are repeated (as aids to recognition?) almost every time they appear. The eighteen occurrences of 'glistening' all apply to Gerald or some part of his anatomy; nothing else in the novel glistens. With Hermione, the words are 'sang' or 'sing-song' (describing her speech) and 'slow/slowly', which is used thirteen times in six pages of chapter 22 to describe her or her actions: 'in her slow voice', 'she said slowly', 'with slow calm eyes', 'Hermione was slow and level', 'with slow pensive eyes', 'Hermione slowly' (three times), 'with her slow heavy gaze', 'in her slow deliberate sing-song', 'slowly she rubbed his head, slowly and with ironic indifference', 'her long slow white fingers'.

But the full effect of Lawrence's repetitions, where they occur in bulk, can only be demonstrated by fairly lengthy quotation; again, a single example from the many must suffice:

'Oh, why wasn't somebody kind to her? Why wasn't there somebody who would take her in their arms, and hold her to their breast, and give her rest, pure, deep, healing rest? Oh, why wasn't there somebody to take her in their arms and fold her safe and perfect, for sleep. She wanted so much this perfect, enfolded sleep. She lay always so unsheathed in sleep. She would lie always unsheathed in sleep, unrelieved, unsaved. Oh, how could she bear it, this endless unrelief, this eternal unrelief?

'Gerald! Could he fold her in his arms and sheathe her in sleep? Ha! He needed putting to sleep himself – poor Gerald! That was all he needed. What did he do, he made the burden greater, the burden of her sleep was the more intolerable, when he was there. He was an added weariness upon her unripening nights, her unfruitful slumbers. Perhaps he got some repose from her. Perhaps he did. Perhaps this was what he was always dogging her for, like a child that is famished, crying for the breast. Perhaps this was the secret of his passion, his for ever unquenched desire for her – that he needed her to put him to sleep, to give him repose.

'What then! Was she his mother? Had she asked for a child, whom she must nurse through the nights for her lover. She despised him, she despised him, she hardened her heart. An infant crying in the night, this Don Juan.

'Ooh, but how she hated the infant crying in the night. She would murder it gladly. She would stifle it and bury it, as Hetty Sorrell did. No doubt Hetty Sorrell's infant cried in the night – no doubt Arthur Donnithorne's would. Ha – the Arthur Donnithornes, the Geralds of this world. So manly by day, yet all the while, such a crying of infants in the night. Let them turn into mechanisms, let them. Let them become instruments, pure machines, pure wills, that work like clockwork, in perpetual repetition. Let them be this, let them be taken up entirely in their work, let them be perfect parts of a great machine, having a slumber of constant repetition. Let Gerald manage his firm. There he would be satisfied, as satisfied as a wheelbarrow that goes backwards and forwards along a plank all day – she had seen it.'[25]

This, with its 'ha's', 'oh's', 'ooh's' and 'what then's', is Lawrence's version of stream-of-consciousness, and it is instructive to compare it with Joyce's. Lawrence's is much less convincing. It is more formal, more stagey, closer to conventional soliloquy; instead of leaping erratically from idea to idea, as the mind does even under stress, it bears down remorselessly on a single line of thought. Moreover, the fact that Gudrun's mannerisms of style, as well as her attitudes to men and machinery, are the same as those Lawrence exhibits in his narrative passages, tends to deprive her of reality as compared with Joyce's individual creations. Not only individual words are repeated – twenty-five of them, some occurring as often as six or eight times – but whole phrases recur either verbatim or with minor modifications, and in addition the same idea is frequently expressed in different words:

'her unripening nights, her unfruitful slumbers'
'his passion, his for ever unquenched desire'
'to put him to sleep, to give him repose,'
'she would murder it . . . she would stifle it.'
'mechanisms . . . instruments, pure machines . . . like clockwork . . . parts of a machine'
'always . . . endless . . . eternal . . . for ever . . . all the while . . . perpetual . . . constant'

The sense of monotony these devices produce is reinforced on the syntactical level. Four consecutive sentences are introduced by 'perhaps', five consecutive clauses by 'let them'; of the thirty-four sentences in the passage,[26] less than a third contain more than a dozen words, half consist of a single main clause only. Still more surprisingly, nearly a quarter of the passage consists of words or phrases in apposition, many of which act as a coda at the ends of sentences: 'pure, deep, healing rest'; 'this endless unrelief, this eternal unrelief'; 'crying for the breast'. (There are eight other instances in the passage.) Here the motivation appears to be phonic, as if Lawrence wished by a series of 'dying falls' to emphasise Gudrun's weariness of Gerald. But the machinery is surely excessive; moreover, the same devices are to be found in such a wide variety of contexts that they can hardly be justified even on grounds of 'expressive form'.

The passages may also be compared with two from *Sons and Lovers* which convey the thoughts and emotions of a solitary character at a moment of psychological stress. The first is where Mrs Morel has been locked out by her husband,[27] the second where Paul reflects on his own situation after his mother's death.[28] The features noted above are almost entirely absent from the first passage, though they begin to make their presence felt in the second. Both passages, however, present a vigour and variety of linguistic resource which contrasts strongly with the narrowness of range in the passage just quoted. And there is another difference. In both the *Sons and Lovers* passages, the central character is planted firmly in the environment; the moonlit garden in which Mrs Morel waits, the starry night through which Paul walks, are evoked vividly in concrete detail. But Gudrun's reflections are given no such local habitation. Of the four hundred words of the extract – indeed of the thousand or so which precede them – not one links her with her surroundings; she exists in a vacuum.

Here is the 'far less visualised' style with a vengeance, and it gives us a clue to another aspect of the novel that has caused some disquiet. Graham Hough admits that most readers 'will find it hard to be convinced by the complicated relations of Gudrun and Gerald, Ursula and Birkin, on the plane of ordinary human action and character', but claims that 'all Lawrence's novels tend to carry more conviction in the ordinary social-naturalist sense the more familiar they become'.[29] This is to admit that they carry little at first – we can get used to anything – and, after many readings, there seems to me still a persistent lack of fit between the actual world and the portrait of it in *Women in Love*; a lack of fit caused by Lawrence's deliberate withdrawal from 'sensation and presentation'.

We can only conclude that Lawrence, in 1913, found himself in the position of Aesop's dog, and dropped the bone of concrete presentation while pursuing the glimmering image of 'deeper strata' and 'allotropic states'. Yet, if language is anything to go by, these states were as difficult to grasp as the reflected bone; and one may well suspect that they had no more reality, and that the 'same single radically unchanged element' into which they could be resolved was none other than Lawrence's own highly idiosyncratic imagination.

Certainly a sense of the author straining over and over again to capture the uncapturable pervades *Women in Love*. It is precisely this straining which produces the inflation and repetition we have noted; and Lawrence, by his acceptance of the ideal of creative spontaneity, by his contemptuous rejection of 'that will of the writer to be greater than and undisputed lord over the stuff he writes, which is figured to the world in Gustave Flaubert',[30] deprived himself of the one means by which he might have corrected such vices of style and made *Women in Love* the great novel which, in conception, it undoubtedly was. For I feel quite certain that its current high estimate needs stringent revision. In spite of all its ingenuity of form, and the many striking scenes it contains, the language in which most of it is written finally leaves one with the feeling that Ursula had while she was watching Birkin playing with daisies:

A strange feeling possessed her, as if something were taking place. But it was all intangible.[31]

SOURCE: essay in *A Review of Engish Literature*, VIII, ii (1967), pp. 56–67.

NOTES

[Renumbered from the original – Ed.]

1. F. R. Leavis, *D. H. Lawrence: Novelist* (1955), pp. 24–5.
2. T. S. Eliot, Foreword to Fr William Tiverton (ed.), *D. H. Lawrence and Human Existence* (1951).
3. John McCormick, *Catastrophe and Imagination* (1957), p. 52.
4. Eliseo Vivas, *D. H. Lawrence: The Failure and the Triumph of Art* (1961), p. 226.
5. Julian Moynahan, *The Deed of Life* (Princeton, 1963), p. 72.
6. Leavis, op. cit., p. 152.
7. *The Letters of D. H. Lawrence*, ed. Harry T. Moore (1962), p. 193.
8. Ibid., p. 282.
9. Ibid., p. 259.
10. Ibid., pp. 183, 203.
11. Graham Hough, *The Dark Sun* (1956), p. 81.
12. Leavis, op. cit., pp. 154–5.
13. D. H. Lawrence, *Women in Love*, Penguin edition (1960), p. 358.
14. F. R. Leavis, 'Revaluations: Joseph Conrad', in *Scrutiny*, X, i (1941), p. 26.
15. *Women in Love*, p. 175.
16. Ibid., p. 19.
17. Ibid., p. 420.
18. Ibid., pp. 214–15.
19. Ibid., p. 345.
20. As many of these words might be used dramatically in dialogue to reveal character, I have counted only those occurrences which are not presented in the form of direct speech. In fact, the phenomenon sometimes described as 'style attraction' – in which dialogue tends to approximate more and more closely to the writer's personal style – is markedly present in the novel, and its growth in Lawrence's work, from *Sons and Lovers* onwards, would also repay study.
21. *Women in Love*, p. 304.
22. Leavis, *D. H. Lawrence*, op. cit., p. 155.
23. D. H. Lawrence, Preface to American Edition of *Women in Love* (1920).
24. *Women in Love*, p. 458.
25. Ibid., pp. 524–5.
26. I have rather arbitrarily taken 'sentence' to mean anything enclosed by full stops, question or exclamation marks. For a linguist's views on 'grammatical' and 'non-grammatical' sentences, see John Spencer, 'A Note on the Steady Monologuy of the Interiors', *Review of English Literature*, VI, 2 (1965), pp. 32–41.
27. D. H. Lawrence, *Sons and Lovers*, Penguin edition (1948), pp. 34–6.
28. Ibid., pp. 509–10.
29. Hough, op. cit., p. 75.

30. D. H. Lawrence, *Selected Literary Criticism*, ed. Anthony Beal (1956), p. 260.

31. *Women in Love*, p. 145.

Anthony Burgess 'The Language of Joyce's *Portrait*' (1973)

. . . In *A Portrait* Joyce is writing only about himself – though we should not assume that the work lacks invention, that Stephen Dedalus is no more than a photograph of his creator. The stylistic problem seems to resolve itself into a need for finding tones, rhythm and lexis appropriate to the young hero at each stage of his growth from infancy to maturity. And so we move from 'baby tuckoo' to a young schoolboy who wonders about adult politics and fails to understand them:

He wondered which was right, to be for the green or for the maroon, because Dante had ripped the green velvet back off the brush that was for Parnell one day with her scissors and had told him that Parnell was a bad man. He wondered if they were arguing at home about that. That was called politics. There were two sides in it: Dante was on one side and his father and Mr Casey were on the other side but his mother and Uncle Charles were on no side.

The simple words, the simple constructions, the naive repetitions are all in order. But, as Stephen grows a little older, subordinate clauses appear, and the vocabulary admits abstractions:

Words which he did not understand he said over and over to himself till he had learnt them by heart; and through them he had glimpses of the real world about him. The hour when he too would take part in the life of that world seemed drawing near and in secret he began to make ready for the great part which he felt awaited him the nature of which he only dimly apprehended.

'The nature of which he only dimly apprehended': evidently Stephen is reading nineteenth-century literature of the staider kind. The movement forward from stage to stage of youth is not smoothly evolutionary: the soul has to be shocked, chiefly through the body, to jerk or jump ahead. Stephen, whose glasses have been broken, is accused of breaking them himself to avoid schoolwork and is beaten by the Prefect of Studies with a pandybat:

A hot burning stinging tingling blow like the loud crack of a broken stick made his trembling hand crumple together lile a leaf in the fire: and at the sound and the pain scalding tears were driven into his eyes. His whole body was shaking with fright, his arm was shaking and his crumpled burning livid hand shook like a loose leaf in the air. A cry sprang to his lips, a prayer to be let off. But though the tears scalded his eyes and his limbs quivered with pain and fright he held back the hot tears and the cry that scalded his throat.
    – Other hand! shouted the prefect of studies.

The power of this is undoubted, but the source of the power is not easy to explain: magic remains a genuine property of art. Still, one ought to observe that much of the excruciating effect springs from objectivity, from an unwillingness to allow the author's own indignation to intrude. Then there is the elemental simplicity of the vocabulary, which emphasises the elemental shock of the pain. There is no finicking attempt to vary the words used: 'scald' appears three times, an apt word worthy to be repeated, since it combines the elements of fire and water. Stephen's passivity is pointed by the two references to his hand as a leaf – once in the fire, once in the third element, air. The pandybat sounds like a stick, but it is a broken stick that could also be in the fire along with the leaf: the experience of pain cannot separate the pain from its cause. The passivity is present in his tears: he does not cry – which seems like performing an action; the tears are 'driven into his eyes'. He does not wish to cry out: the cry springs to his lips. The onomatopoeic effects need hardly be commented on. Repeated vowels and consonants express the noise of the pandybat, but the manner in which the agony of the blow seems to take possession of the entire universe is conveyed by the swift vocalic leaps, as though the pain were rushing from the centre to all possible spatial positions.

Thus, in the first sentence, we dart from the back round close vowel in 'hot' to the slack central vowel of 'burning,' then up to the high front slack vowel which is used five times successively, back to the round diphthong of 'blow', down to the rising diphthong of 'like', and so on. The sentence contains all the vowels except /aɪ/ and /uː/, five diphthongs, and the triphthong (though this may not be in everyone's phonemic inventory) in 'fire.' This is not in itself remarkable, but the manner in which diverse tongue-and-lip positions are juxtaposed certainly gives a ghastly vigour to the passage.

The technique of *Ulysses* is foreshadowed at two points in the narrative of the chapter where Stephen is mature enough to have fallen into deep sin and experiences spiritual torments which breed hallucinations. Faces watch him and voices murmur:

– We knew perfectly well of course that although it was bound to come to the light he would find considerable difficulty in endeavouring to try to induce himself to try to endeavour to ascertain the spiritual plenipotentiary and so we knew of course perfectly well –

The vision of hell is almost a stage direction from 'Circe':

A field of stiff weeds and thistles and tufted nettlebunches. Thick among the tufts of rank stiff growth lay battered canisters and clots and coils of solid excrement. A faint marsh light struggling upwards from all the ordure through the bristling greygreen weeds. An evil smell, faint and foul as the light, curled upwards sluggishly out of the canisters and from the stale crusted dung.

We note here what we will note in *Ulysses*: Joyce's preference for a compound word over a noun-phrase ('nettlebunches' instead of 'bunches of nettles'); his liking for an adjective-phrase followed by inversion of subject and verb ('Thick among the tufts of rank stiff growth lay battered canisters . . .'); his insistence on a vocabulary of Anglo-Saxon origin when presenting material directed at the senses. ('Canister' is from Latin *canistrum*; its use here is probably part-dictated by the ecclesiastical connotation, since a canister is the vessel that holds the wafers before they are consecrated. 'Excrement' is preferred to *shit* or *shite*, but Joyce intends to make the latter word express the ultimate nausea of the vision.) Again, the prosodic technique is masterly. The 'clotted' effect partly derives from the double consonants – /ld/, /dz/, /ft/, /nʃ/ and so on – and occasional triple consonants: /slz/, /fts/, /kskr/ in 'excrement' (a tougher word than any Anglo-Saxon equivalent).

When Stephen emerges into the fair fields of penitent purity, the prose becomes unexpectedly pedestrian, to match the failure of the young soul to find the ecstasy it hoped for in virtue and mortification of the flesh:

He seemed to feel his soul in devotion pressing like fingers the keyboard of a great cash register and to see the amount of his purchase start forth immediately in heaven, not as a number but as a frail column of incense or as a slender flower.

But when he realises that his vocation is to be a sinning artist, he has a new vision, that of a winged form over the sea, slowly mounting the sky – his protonym Daedalus, the fabulous artificer. The prose that conveys his ecstatic state balances the Anglo-Saxon and Latin elements of English; the syntax becomes simple, almost childish, to match the sense of being newborn:

His heart trembled in an ecstasy of fear and his soul was in flight. His soul was soaring in an air beyond the world and the body he knew was purified in a breath and delivered of incertitude and made radiant and commingled with the element of the spirit. An ecstasy of flight made radiant his eyes and wild his breath and tremulous and wild and radiant his windswept limbs.

This is expressive of a somewhat immature transport: after all, Stephen is still a schoolboy. It is the prose appropriate to a youth who has read Shelley but is not yet ready for either Donne or Rabelais.

The final section of the novel, in which Stephen is presented as a rebellious undergraduate unsympathetic to philistine, religiose Ireland, a fierce young artist and aesthetic philosopher who has left the Church and is preparing to leave the country, anticipates stylistically the first chapter of *Ulysses*. The important things are less what Stephen does than what he says; we come close to monologue, in which the outside world that has menaced him so long is at last enclosed and tamed by his mind. It is at the end of the novel that we realise how thoroughgoing Joyce's objectivity has been. The mature artist has never once stepped in to qualify the attitudes of the young soul struggling unconsciously towards a vocation. The undergraduate Stephen is old enough for the creator Joyce to be tempted into an identification, but the mind that is brilliant enough for the disquisition on aesthetics is also adolescent enough for *fin-de-siècle* postures of 'weariness' and for a brash unlikeable dogmatism that Joyce neither condones nor condemns. The book ends with diary entries which, in their elliptical irritability, self-mockery, fearless lyricism, look forward to the 'Proteus' episode of *Ulysses*, but, in their lack of syntax and flashes of discrete observation, recall the opening with 'baby tuckoo' and his attempts to make a gestalt out of smells and hot and cold and wet and dry. The cutting of the physical umbilical cord is matched by the cutting of the spiritual. 'Welcome, O life!' cries the artist as a young man, and he goes forth 'to forge in the smithy of my soul the uncreated conscience of my race'. . . .

SOURCE: extract from *Joysprick: An Introduction to the Language of James Joyce* (London, 1973), pp. 65–9.

John Russell Brown 'The Language of Harold Pinter' (1972)

. . . No detail of Pinter's writing can be adequately considered outside the context of the complete drama in which it must play its part. But by examining some short passages, his continuous control may be seen at work, and his awareness of the part words play in dramatic confrontations of considerable complexity but little explicit verbal statement. The more recurrent devices of language illustrate the nature of his perception and the means whereby he ensures that that perception is communicated in his writing.

The most difficult to describe is Pinter's manipulation of

rhythms. Speeches run in one kind of phrasing, until some subtextual pressure lengthens, shortens or quickens the utterance and so, by sound alone, betrays the change of engagement. The last episode of *The Birthday Party* illustrates this:

[MEG *comes past the window and enters by the back door.* PETEY *studies the front page of the paper.*]

MEG [*coming downstage*]: The car's gone.

PETEY: Yes.

MEG: Have they gone?

PETEY: Yes.

MEG: Won't they be in for lunch?

PETEY: No.

MEG: Oh, what a shame. [*She puts her bag on the table.*] It's hot out. [*She hangs her coat on a hook.*] What are you doing?

PETEY: Reading.

MEG: Is it good?

PETEY: All right.

   [*She sits by the table.*]

MEG: Where's Stan?

   [*Pause.*]

Is Stan down yet, Petey?

PETEY: No . . . He's . . .

MEG: Is he still in bed?

PETEY: Yes, he's . . . still asleep.

MEG: Still? He'll be late for his breakfast.

PETEY: Let him . . . sleep.

   [*Pause.*]

MEG: Wasn't it a lovely party last night?

PETEY: I wasn't there.

MEG: Weren't you?

PETEY: I came in afterwards.

MEG: Oh.

   [*Pause.*]

It was a lovely party. I haven't laughed so much for years. We had dancing and singing. And games. You should have been there.

PETEY: It was good, eh?

   [*Pause.*]

MEG: I was the belle of the ball.

PETEY: Were you?

MEG: Oh yes. They all said I was.

PETEY: I bet you were, too.

MEG: Oh, it's true. I was.

   [*Pause.*]

I know I was.   CURTAIN

Meg's first three speeches have two main stresses each, the third containing a greater number of unstressed syllables; then, as she registers Petey's 'No', the rhythm changes, starting with a single syllable 'Oh', and then after a comma three more, the middle one being unstressed: 'Oh, what a shame.' She then moves about the room and begins speech again in much the same rhythms as at first. But when Petey replies this time, the phrasing grows shorter: 'Is it good?' and then, having sat down, a simple two-stressed, two-syllabled 'Where's Stan?'. At this point there is a '*Pause*' during which her energy changes rhythm, for there now comes a slightly longer question, less emphatic, and 'Petey' at the end following a comma's pause: 'Is Stan down yet, Petey?' When Petey answers with broken phrasing and hesitation 'No . . . he's . . . ', she first gains speed – 'Is he still in bed?' – with light front vowels and no more than two stresses. But she then seems to halt with a monosyllabic question (that repeats 'still' for the second time), but soon runs on with her observation, 'He'll be late for his breakfast'. This assumption of knowledge seems to allow her to change the whole mood of her thoughts, for a pause is now of her making; and when she speaks again, the rhythm is almost lilting, as if she were happily lost in idle thoughts: 'Wasn't it a lovely party last night?' Petey's disclaimer breaks the mood momentarily, but after another pause, again of her own making, she picks up with a longer speech that has varied rhythms within it. The rhythmical jingle of '. . . dancing and singing' is followed by the shorter and slightly disturbing rhythm of a short, verbless sentence 'And games'; this alludes to the frightening part of the evening. But then, as she remembers Petey was not there, the tension is again relaxed. Meg's final speeches begin again with a dreamy ease: 'I was the belle of the ball'; but Petey's question and then his support tighten the rhythms. Her reply to the question starts with a two-syllable assertion, 'Oh yes', and then a rather longer agreement, 'They all said I was'. Her reply to his token of support is short but with two pauses, the first slight and the second more emphatic: 'Oh, it's true. I was.' A '*Pause*' follows and then her last speech with two very short elements and a repeated 'I', in its single phrase: 'I know I was.' The rhythm of this last utterance is short, contained and simple; and, since 'know' carries more stress than 'was', it has a slight falling-off. This tightening of the rhythms of speech is all the more effective for contrast with the lighter rhythms and longer reach of her preceding speeches.

Petey's rhythms start with stark monosyllables: 'Yes . . . Yes . . . No.' When Meg returns to the attack, they are less firm with two-syllables: 'Reading . . . All right', the second giving an abrupt sound in comparison with the light ending of the first. When he is questioned about Stanley, his rhythms are broken, finding their firmest point on the concluding monosyllable, 'sleep'. Petey's next replies seem light, unstressed and smooth in comparison, as if yielding even as he contradicts Meg. When she enters her reverie, he seems to give light compliance with 'It was good, eh?' and 'I bet you were, too', each with a single syllable after a brief pause at the end of the line. The strongest contrast here is in the two-syllabled 'Were you?' that could be delivered slowly or a little weighted.

The two characters have their own rhythms that are shown off by varied contrasts throughout the episode. But there is one point where they seem to speak almost in the same 'breath', with a similar shortness of phrase, though with varying emphasis. This is when Petey's answers grow to 'Reading' and 'All right', and Meg shortens her questions to 'Is it good?' and then 'Where's Stan?' This rhythmic 'meeting' may represent an unspoken acknowledgement of the one urgent matter they must both learn to face and live with. It lasts for only a moment that continues into the pause; then Meg's uncertainty forces the pace again.

If only the sounds of the words were heard, or if the dialogue was followed by someone not knowing a word of English, much of the pressures, tactics and moments of decision in this episode would be communicated. Such response might be more valid and exciting than if a reader registered the words without recreating their sound in his mind as well as registering their implications. Sound and the interplay of rhythms are constant factors in the effectiveness of Pinter's dialogue. . . .

SOURCE: extract from *Theatre Language* (London, 1972), pp. 34–8.

SELECT BIBLIOGRAPHY

The following are recommended for further reading and consultation. Additional references will be found in the notes to the Introduction.

Richard W. Bailey and Dolores M. Burton, *English Stylistics: A Bibliography* (Cambridge, Mass., 1968).

Owen Barfield, *Poetic Diction: A Study in Meaning* (London, 1928; rev. edn., 1952).

F. W. Bateson, *The Scholar–Critic* (London, 1972).

Christine Brooke-Rose, *A Grammar of Metaphor* (London, 1958).

Raymond Chapman, *Linguistics and Literature* (London, 1973).

S. B. Chatman (ed.), *Literary Style: A Symposium* (London, 1971).

Ann Cluysenaar, *Introduction to Literary Stylistics* (London, 1976).

David Crystal and Derek Davy, *Investigating English Style* (London, 1969).

L. Dolezel and R. W. Bailey, *Statistics and Style* (New York, 1969).

Roger Fowler, *Linguistics and the Novel* (London, 1977).

Roger Fowler (ed.), *Essays on Style and Language* (London, 1966).

Donald C. Freeman, (ed.), *Linguistics and Literary Style* (New York, 1970).

Geoffrey Leech, *A Linguistic Guide to English Poetry* (London, 1969).

C. S. Lewis, *Studies in Words* (Cambridge, 1960).

F. L. Lucas, *Style* (London, 1955).

John Middleton Murry, *The Problem of Style* (Oxford, 1922).

Randolph Quirk, *The Use of English* (London, 1968).

Herbert Read, *English Prose Style* (London, 1928).

Susie I. Tucker, *Protean Shape: A Study in Eighteenth-Century Vocabulary and Usage* (London, 1967).

G. W. Turner, *Stylistics* (Harmondsworth, 1973).

Stephen Ullmann, *Meaning and Style* (Oxford, 1964).

Austin Warren and René Wellek, *Theory of Literature* (New York, 1949).

George Watson (ed.), *Literary English Since Shakespeare* (London, 1970).

Leslie Fiedler "Archetype & Signature"

NOTES ON CONTRIBUTORS

JOSEPH ADDISON (1672–1719): periodical essayist, poet and dramatist.

MATTHEW ARNOLD (1822–88): poet, critic and educationist.

F. W. BATESON (1901–78): formerly University Lecturer in English Literature at Oxford and Fellow of Corpus Christi College; he founded and edited the periodical *Essays in Criticism*, and edited the *Cambridge Bibliography of English Literature* (1940).

FRANCIS BERRY (born 1915): formerly Professor of English Language and Literature, Royal Holloway College, University of London; his publications include *Poetry and the Physical Voice* (1962) and various volumes of verse.

DEREK BICKERTON has taught at the universities of Leeds and Guyana; his publications include *Dynamics of a Creole System* (1975).

CLEANTH BROOKS (born 1906): Gray Professor of Rhetoric at Yale University; in addition to *The Well Wrought Urn* (1947), his publications include two books on William Faulkner; he co-edited (1935–42) the influential periodical *Southern Review*.

JOHN RUSSELL BROWN (born 1923): Professor of English, Sussex University; his publications include *Shakespeare and his Comedies* (1957), *Shakespeare's Dramatic Style* (1970), *Free Shakespeare* (1974), *Discovering Shakespeare* (1981) and edited volumes in the Casebook series.

ANTHONY BURGESS (born 1917): novelist and critic; his critical works include *The Novel Today* (1963) and *Here Comes Everybody: An Introduction to James Joyce* (1965).

SAMUEL TAYLOR COLERIDGE (1772–1834): poet and critic.

JONATHAN CULLER (born 1944): Professor of English and Comparative Literature at Cornell University; his publications include *Flaubert: The Uses of Uncertainty* (1974), *Structuralist Poetics* (1975) and *Ferdinand de Saussure* (1976).

DONALD DAVIE (born 1922): Andrew W. Mellon Professor of Humanities, Vanderbilt University; his publications include *Purity of Diction in English Verse* (1952), *Thomas Hardy and British Poetry* (1972), and *Collected Poems* (1972).

T. S. ELIOT (1888–1965): poet, dramatist, and critic; his critical writings include *The Sacred Wood* (1920) and *Selected Essays* (1932).

WILLIAM EMPSON (born 1906): Emeritus Professor of English Literature, Sheffield University, and Honorary Fellow of Magdalene College, Cambridge; his publications include *Some Versions of Pastoral* (1935), *The Structure of Complex Words* (1951), *Milton's God* (1961) and *Collected Poems* (1955).

THOMAS GRAY (1716–71): poet and letter-writer.

MICHAEL GREGORY: Professor of English, Glendon College, Toronto; his publications include essays on linguistics and stylistics.

BERNARD GROOM, formerly Professor of English Language and Literature, University of Montevideo; his publications include *A Short History of English Words* (1949) and *The Unity of Wordsworth's Poetry* (1966).

A. E. HOUSMAN (1859–1936): poet and classical scholar; *The Name and Nature of Poetry* was originally given in 1933 as the Leslie Stephen Lecture at Cambridge.

RANDALL JARRELL (1914–65): American poet, novelist and critic. His critical works include *Poetry and the Age* (1953) and *A Sad Heart at the Supermarket* (1962).

SAMUEL JOHNSON (1709–84): poet, prose writer, lexicographer, biographer, and editor of Shakespeare.

F. R. LEAVIS (1895–1978): formerly Fellow of Downing College, Cambridge, University Reader in English at Cambridge, and visiting Professor at York University; his publications include *New Bearings in English Poetry* (1932), and *The Great Tradition* (1948).

VERNON LEE (pseudonym of Violet Paget, 1856–1935): novelist and essayist.

DAVID LODGE (born 1935): Professor of Modern English Literature, Birmingham University; his publications include *The Novelist at the Crossroads* (1971), *The Modes of Modern Writing* (1977), several novels, and the volume on *Emma* in the Casebook series.

ANGUS McINTOSH (born 1914): formerly Forbes Professor of English Language, University of Edinburgh, and now Director of the Middle English Dialect Atlas Project; he is the co-author (with M. A. K. Halliday) of *Patterns of Language* (1966).

M. M. MAHOOD: until her retirement she was Professor of English at the University of Kent; her publications include *Poetry and Humanism* (1950) and *Joyce Cary's Africa* (1964).

SYLVÈRE MONOD: Professor of English at The Sorbonne; in addition to *Dickens the Novelist* (1968) he has published many essays on Victorian fiction, and has translated some of Dickens's novels into French.

WINIFRED NOWOTTNY: formerly Reader in English at University College, London; *The Language Poets Use* (1962) is her most important work.

NORMAN PAGE (born 1930): Professor of English, University of Alberta; his publications include *Thomas Hardy* (1977), *A. E. Housman: A Critical Biography* (1983), *A Dickens Companion* (1983), and the volume on *Hard Times*, *Great Expectations* and *Our Mutual Friend* in the Casebook series.

ALEXANDER POPE (1688–1744): poet and satirist.

I. A. RICHARDS (1893–1979): he taught at Cambridge and Harvard, and in China: his publications include *Practical Criticism* (1929) and (with C. K. Ogden) *The Meaning of Meaning* (1923).

CHRISTOPHER RICKS (born 1933): King Edward VII Professor of English Literature at Cambridge; his publications include *Tennyson* (1972) and *Keats and Embarrassment* (1974).

JOHN RUSKIN (1819–1900): critic and moralist.

SIR PHILIP SIDNEY (1554–86): poet and prose writer.

JOHN SPENCER: Senior Lecturer in English, University of Leeds; his publications include many essays on linguistics and stylistics.

CAROLINE SPURGEON (1869–1942): her publications include *Keats's Shakespeare* (1928) and *Leading Motives in the Imagery of Shakespeare's Tragedies* (1930).

GEORGE RYLANDS (born 1902): formerly Fellow of King's College, Cambridge, and University Lecturer in English; his publications include *Shakespeare's Poetic Energy* (1951).

GEORGE WATSON (born 1927): Fellow of St John's College, Cambridge, and University Lecturer in English; his publications include *The Literary Critics* (1962), *Coleridge the Poet* (1966), *The Discipline of English* (1978) and *The Story of the Novel* (1979) and he has edited *The New Cambridge Bibliography of English Literature*.

STANLEY WELLS (born 1930): Head of the Shakespeare Department, Oxford University Press, and General Editor of the Oxford Shakespeare; his publications include *Shakespeare: The Writer and his Work* (1978), and he is editor of the annual *Shakespeare Survey*.

WILLIAM WORDSWORTH (1770–1850): poet and poetic theorist.

INDEX

READER'S NOTES